D1715127

Fly Patterns of Yellowstone

Fly Patterns of Yellowstone

by
CRAIG MATHEWS
and
JOHN JURACEK

First Published 1987 by
Blue Ribbon Flies
West Yellowstone, MT 59758
© Craig Mathews, John Juracek 1987
Printed in U.S.A.

Contents

Acknowledgements

We would like to give a special thank-you to the following people:

Verlyn Klinkenborg, Nick Lyons, and Tom Young, all of whom provided valuable criticisms, comments, and suggestions on the manuscript.

Ken Takata, whose excellent photographs add greatly to the book.

Fred Harrison, whose constant encouragement and support mean a great deal to us.

Jackie Mathews, who typed more than her share of the manuscript.

And thanks to all the Yellowstone flyfishers who over the course of many seasons have influenced our views of flies and fly tying.

Preface

A guidebook to Yellowstone fly patterns has been long overdue. While much has been written about Yellowstone area waters the question "What flies do I need?" has remained largely unanswered. We feel this book can provide answers to that question, and furnish helpful fishing and fly tying ideas along the way.

Any list of flies is subjective, of course, and often parallels the fishing style and preferred waters of its author. We believe this book's flies reflect the varied water that can be found in the Yellowstone area. Whether you fish lakes, rivers, ponds, or small streams, the following flies can help make your Yellowstone fishing experience more enjoyable. They have worked for us and we are sure they will work for you.

Pheasant Tail Nymph

Frank Sawyer's Pheasant Tail Nymph is one of those rare flies that performs double duty: it is both imitative and suggestive and is superb when used for either purpose. Sawyer tied it to imitate the *Baetis* mayfly nymphs of England, though by his own admission much of the P.T.'s success was attributable to the fact that it could be mistaken, in different sizes, for many other species of fly. It is his most famous fly, and in "*Nymphs and the Trout*" he felt sure the fly would "continue to hold pride of place as an effective artificial" throughout the world. The popularity of the P.T. in the Yellowstone area alone buttresses his contention.

Sawyer felt the fly imitated a dozen or so English mayfly species and such is the case in our area. In fact, the P.T. effectively imitates well over a dozen important mayflies in Yellowstone country. There isn't a trout stream around here that doesn't contain some natural mayfly whose nymph isn't matched by the Pheasant tail; consequently it should be the basic nymph choice for fishing out here.

We fish it blind before a hatch, to specific fish during a hatch if the fish are nymphing, and as an attractor during most of the summer months. It should be dressed weighted (as Sawyer did, using copper wire in place of tying thread) and unweighted, as in this slight modification of the pattern. Both versions are important to have, depending on where and how the fly is fished.

Our favorite hatches and rivers to fish this fly? The Firehole in June during the Pale Morning Dun emergence, late September on the Yellowstone, imitating the Blue Winged Olive nymphs, and during October on the Madison, using it to suggest the prolific *Baetis* mayflies. A truly versatile fly.

The P.T. is also a simple fly to tie. Sawyer tied it using copper wire as the thread, both to add weight to the fly and to create a pronounced thorax. After building up the front of the hook with wraps of wire, the pheasant fibers were tied on to form a short tail and then wrapped up the hook to form the body and thorax. The wingcase was shaped by lapping the remaining ends of the pheasant fibers back and forth over the thorax, finally tying off at the eye.

The version we have shown incorporates peacock herl for the thorax, and is unweighted. Tie in the tips of the pheasant fibers to form a short tail, wind them up the hook shank, and anchor the fibers where the thorax will start. Do not trim the remainder of the fibers, as they will be used to create the wingcase. Tie in and wind the peacock to form the thorax. After trimming the excess peacock, pull the strands of pheasant over the top of the thorax and tie off at the eye.

Pheasant Tail Nymph

HOOK:	Mustad 94840 or equivalent, #14-#20.
THREAD:	6/0 brown.
TAIL:	Four cock ringneck pheasant tail fibers.
BODY:	Same pheasant tail fibers, wrapped on hook shank.
THORAX:	Two strands of peacock herl.
WINGCASE:	Same four original pheasant fibers, pulled over the top.

Fur Nymph

The need for a suggestive nymph pattern that can be fished dry, semi-dry, or just under the surface will become apparent to almost any angler once he acquires a certain amount of experience in fishing mayfly hatches. On many occasions trout will forsake the duns in favor of the more easily captured emerging nymphs, though it is impossible to predict accurately when this will happen.

Most likely a host of factors contribute to the trout's decision to take nymphs, some of which seem to be the following: species of mayfly, species of trout, size of the trout, wind, temperature, relative quantities of nymph and dun available at any given time, overall intensity of the hatch, position of fish within the stream, etc. Precisely how these factors relate to each other is difficult to say, though it would certainly be interesting to know instead of relying on speculation. Ultimately we can probably just assume that when it is advantageous, in terms of energy conservation, for a fish to feed on nymphs instead of duns it will do so; when the reverse is true, it will choose duns and ignore the nymphs.

Correctly interpreting a riseform that originated from the taking of a nymph and not a dun can be quite challenging, but it is a valuable skill. It calls for close attention to both the water and the fish. Some things we have found helpful are: 1) watch individual duns floating by, and see if they are being picked off (a dun feeding indication) or are passing by while the fish still feed (probably nymph feeding), 2) study the fish carefully when they rise; are noses and heads breaking water (probably dun feeding), just backs and tails, or just tails alone? (both good indications of nymph feeding), and 3) know, or ask someone who knows, the characteristics of the particular mayfly that's hatching. Are the nymphs important, do the fish have a tendency to feed on them, etc. Knowledge of the life history of a mayfly is often overlooked, but it can provide many clues that directly increase fishing success.

This fur nymph pattern represents a style of fly as well as imitating several different species of mayfly. This particular fly is especially useful for imitating the Pale Morning Duns, but with a change of color it can represent many other important species. As unpretentious as it is, getting it to look right can be tricky. Start the tying by attaching the three partridge fiber tails. Then begin dubbing the body using rather coarse fur such as Australian oppossum. It should taper gradually, tail to head, and also become quite fuzzy in the thorax area. This is accomplished by dubbing roughly or using a dubbing needle to pick out the fur. The correct look is one with enough definition to clearly represent a nymph, but fuzzy enough to really suggest "life". The hairs sticking out also make this fly, when dressed with floatant, unsinkable. Without dressing it fishes right in the film.

Fur Nymph

HOOK: Mustad 94840 or equivalent, #14-#22.
THREAD: 6/0 brown or olive.
TAIL: Three partridge fibers.
BODY: Australian opposum, seal, or other coarse dubbing to match naturals. We like dark brown and pale olive.
THORAX: Same as body, dubbed rough or picked out.

Peacock

When Dave Schultz first tied up this little nymph at our tying bench, he said what we always hear from fishermen: use this when all else fails.

And, of course, it was not until all else did fail that we reached for this fly, having kept it on hand only out of respect for Dave's fishing wisdom. A September *Paraleptophlebia* (Mahogany Dun) hatch on the Henry's Fork with the rainbows pursuing emerging nymphs was the first instance that proved the effectiveness of this fly to us.

Later, during a mixed October hatch of Blue Winged Olives and *Baetis* on the Yellowstone, when the cutthroats nymphed exclusively in the film, this fly was without peer. The same fish that three months earlier would attack almost any fly cast to them had become notoriously picky and difficult during the last hatches of the season. It was, and still is every year, extremely challenging fishing. The Peacock in sizes #18 and #22, fished dead drift to individual fish, was never refused. Its power of attraction seemed almost mystical.

Our final test was an end of the season *Baetis* hatch on the Madison: fascinating fishing to actively feeding pocket water trout. During this hatch the largest fish invariably feed on nymphs in the current seams, rarely rising to take the tiny duns, but rolling, tailing, and porpoising wantonly in pursuit of the nymphs. Such was the scene when we decided to break out the Peacock in sizes #20 and #22. For several hours it put on a capital performance, again fished upstream dead drift just under the surface to individual fish.

Many fishermen have long believed there is something about peacock herl (color, irridescence, etc.) that makes it irresistible to fish. Since herl is the sole material in this fly, perhaps there is some substance to their claims.

There may not be an easier fly to tie either; just wrap peacock herl on a hook and whip finish. If you like, reinforce the herl with tying thread for a more durable fly. We prefer to trim the peacock lightly to give a slight front to back taper.

Peacock

HOOK: Mustad 94840 or equivalent, #14-#22.
BODY: Peacock herl wrapped, then trimmed.
THREAD: 6/0 olive.

Green Drake Emerger

Late June on the Henry's Fork is a magic time. This is the time of year when the Green Drake mayflies emerge daily and bring to the surface some of the largest fish in the river. Anglers gather from all parts of the country for their chance at a big one. For many, the yearly trip to the Henry's Fork at this time is almost a religious rite: Mecca manifested as a river and its fish!

The Green Drake is a powerful stimulus to both fish and fishermen. For fishermen, their emergence evokes strong emotions. They either love the flies or hate them. Unfortunately, much of the dislike being voiced about the Green Drake is, we suspect, misdirected. If the truth be known, the criticisms usually stem more from the numbers of fishermen present than from the insects themselves. After all, what's not to like about a fly that brings the real monsters out in the open to feed freely? The Green Drakes can do this to the big fish, and sometimes rather blatantly at that.

Two years ago on the Henry's Fork we happened on a big bank sipper rising to the remnants of the day's Green Drake activity. Most anglers had already begun heading in for the afternoon, walking carelessly up the bank, and, as it turned out, many were passing within fifteen feet of this fish. After a good hatch it is always possible to find trout that have moved in close to the bank to feed on any straggling duns that the current brings along. Now, following other fishermen who are walking up the bank is not our favorite, nor an especially effective tactic for spotting these fish, but during the rather crowded Green Drake time it can still pay to keep an eye out. Even with that in mind it was a great surprise to happen across this fish, working so close to where the fishermen were trodding. Obviously he was more intent on dining on Green Drakes than exercising the caution trout of his size normally do.

After a downstream approach and about a dozen casts (to his credit he was at least in a funny little eddy), he rose confidently to the emerger. A determined, if somewhat unspectacular, fight followed and he was shortly brought to hand. It was a rare and beautiful rainbow, measuring an even twenty-six inches.

With any insect, witnessing an emergence and watching the struggle for flight is an impressive sight, but the Green Drake's sheer size and ungraceful behavior make a fisherman, on occasion, really start rooting for them, hoping they get off the water and to the bank safely rather than suffering an untimely death in the jaws of a big rainbow or a passing bird.

Being rather clumsy mayflies, the Drakes also suffer a lot of casualties during actual hatching. They get stuck halfway out of the shuck, many emerge deformed and unable to fly, and even when they do escape the shuck it takes them a long time to get their wings straightened around and ready for flying. As they float downstream they tip over a lot too, ending up pinned to the surface and an easy meal for a trout.

All these characteristics and positions are well suggested by the Green Drake Emerger, and it is generally considered the best choice of fly for fishing the hatch. Fished dry it is almost never refused by a fish eating naturals. It is a great fly to fish during the one to two week period when the hatch is on even if no naturals are on the water at all. The trout get locked in on them and can't refuse an imitation of a disheveled looking Drake. The moose tail gives the impression of a trailing shuck, the swept back hackle suggests deformed, awash, or otherwise impaired wings, and the whole fly floats low in the water just like a natural in trouble. Incidentally, during those rare times a Drake spinner fall is encountered, this fly doubles beautifully as a spinner imitation.

Tying the Emerger is quite easy. Begin by anchoring a tail of moose to the hook, half the length of the body. Tie in a length of yellow polyester thread. Dub a body of olive fur to behind the eye, being sure to leave room for the hackle. Wind the ribbing thread in even spirals. Then tie in and wind a dyed saddle or neck hackle, folding the hackle as it is wound to force the fibers into a swept-back position. This is the desired look, and folding the hackle eliminates the need to wind back over the hackle with thread to force the hackle back. Whip finish to form a small head.

Green Drake Emerger

HOOK:	Mustad 94831 or equivalent, #10-#12.
THREAD:	6/0 olive or yellow.
TAIL:	Moose body hair.
BODY:	Olive dubbing.
RIB:	Yellow polyester thread.
HACKLE:	Grizzly dyed yellowish olive.

Green Drake Paradrake

This paradrake fly is a popular and very realistic imitation of the adult Green Drake mayfly. Though its opportunities for use may be more limited than those for the emerger pattern, it still maintains an appropriate place as an effective pattern.

If we had to choose between the paradrake and the emerger, basing the decision solely on effectiveness, our vote would be cast for the emerger. However, there are often other factors to consider, some of which weigh more heavily than a slight difference in effectiveness. The paradrake is a much easier fly to see on the water because it has an upright wing and tends to float a little better than the emerger. For many fishermen this increased visibility makes it a more valuable and effective fly under all conditions. For others the paradrake's visibility and flotation make a difference only when fishing faster, choppier water conditions. Let's not forget that Green Drakes aren't found only in smooth water; besides the rougher water sections of the Henry's Fork (the best known Green Drake river), Green Drake hatches can be found on the Yellowstone River, the Lamar River, Soda Butte Creek, Slough Creek, the Lewis River and occasionally even on the Madison River below Quake Lake, a classic piece of pocket water. When visibility and flotation are the most important factors, the paradrake is often a better choice of fly.

Tying the paradrake is complicated and requires experience as well as patience to do the job right. Begin by tying on the wing, making it slightly taller and positioning it slightly further back on the hook than for a normal hairwing pattern. Note the photograph. Wrap Monocord around the base of the wing where the parachute hackle will be wound; this provides a foundation for the hackle to anchor on. Next tie on the hackle so that it stands upright right alongside the wing. The tail follows, and judging the proper length is somewhat a matter of style. Just remember that there is an extended body on this fly, so the tail must be longer than normal to allow for the longer body. Five strands of moose should be tied in to start. Advance the thread to the eye of the hook, making sure a good thread base covers the shank. Tie on a clump of dyed elk at the hook eye, with the tips facing out over the eye. The butts should be trimmed where they meet the wing. The correct amount of elk to use will take some trial and error to determine; some tiers like a thick body, others a thin one, so personal preference plays a part too.

With the Monocord immediately in front of the wing, pull the dyed elk backwards toward the tail, forming a bullet head that completely surrounds the hook with no loose fibers. Keeping hold of the elk, begin wrapping the Monocord by taking three or four turns on top of each other in front of the wing and then making nice even spirals to the bend of the hook and then off the hook to form the extended body. Make sure the tail fibers are enclosed in the clump of elk. Wind the Monocord back in tight even spirals to just in front of the wing. Now wrap the hackle. The first turn of hackle should be the highest on the wing, with each succeeding turn positioned just below the previous one. When there is no more space for further turns, tie off and whip finish just in front of the wing. Trim the excess elk fibers off that form the body, being careful not to cut the tails. Finally trim off two of the tails, leaving three behind, and apply head cement at the rear of the body and the point where the hackle is tied off.

Green Drake Paradrake

HOOK: Mustad 94840 or equivalent, #10-#12.
THREAD: 3/0 yellow Monocord.
WING: Dyed gray elk or deer hair.
HACKLE: Grizzly dyed yellowish olive.
TAIL: Moose body hair.
BODY: Dyed olive elk hair.

Sparkle Dun

Here is one of our own patterns which has proven successful all over the world. We have used it for all major Yellowstone area mayfly emergences with great results. The pattern works well when the trout are nymphing, taking emergers, stillborns, or duns, and often even spinners.

It's easy to tie, durable, uses inexpensive materials and best of all it is extremely effective.

The "sparkle" in the Sparkle Dun comes from the

sparkle poly used for the shuck or tail portion of this fly. We make mention here of the fact this material is sparkle poly yarn and *not* antron.

This is a most adaptable pattern - it even performs well on hatches such as Gray Drakes when no dun pattern should really work since the duns emerge on shore out of the water.

The evolution of this fly is interesting. We had used stillborn patterns as first tied by Swisher and Richards with limited success. One morning while observing emerging Pale Morning Duns at the crossover fence to the Harriman Ranch on the Henry's Fork we noted a great number of stillborns coming down in the drift. Most stillborns were still attached to the nymphal shuck which sparkled and shimmered in the light. The shuck while still attached to the abdomen trapped the tails or legs of the duns. We felt that this sparkle-shimmering feature of the still attached shuck may have been the "trigger" to the rise for these stillborns.

Combining a wing of deer hair for durability, a dubbed body, and a sparkle poly nymphal shuck, we created a pattern which is easy to tie, floats well, is visible, and produces better than other no-hackle designs or stillborn imitations we have tried. The sparkle poly seems to be the key to this flies effectiveness; it imitates the shuck better than any other material we've tried.

The deer for the wing should be hollow well up into the tips because the wing must flare like a fan for stability and to provide the proper silhouette. The thread should sink into the hair when wrapped on the hook shank. There is then less bulk behind the wing, allowing for a neater, more realistic silhouette.

We cannot stress enough that the fly tyer obtain the right piece of deer hair for this pattern. Deer mask is *not* the right material — most of it is not hollow, will bulk up, will not flare and will not float. Some leg hair is acceptable but the tier's best bet is to find a piece with short tips off a western whitetail deer killed in September or October. The sides of the neck and upper legs above the knee are the best locations of the hide to obtain hair for

Sparkle Duns. When thumb nail pressure is applied at the tie-in point of the hair it should easily flare and compress. Usually coarser hair is preferred over fine because it is hollow and possesses the qualities mentioned above.

For Yellowstone area mayfly hatches we fish the Sparkle Dun during the following emergences:

Pale Morning Duns (*Ephemerella infrequens* and
inermis)
Tiny Western Olives (*Baetis species*)
Mahogany Duns (*Paraleptophlebia species*)
White Wing Blacks (*Tricorythodes minutus*)
Speckled Spinners (*Callibaetis species*)
Small Green Drakes (*Drunella flavilinea* and
coloradensis)
Blue Wing Olives (*Attenella margarita*)

Tying the Sparkle Dun is easy with the correct materials. Begin with the wing, tying it in with the tips extending over the hook eye; length of wing equal to the length of the hook shank. The wing is then forced into an upright position by pulling it up and wrapping tying thread in front of the base; *forcing* the wing to stand upright. *Do not* wait to force the wing up with dubbing as it will only creep forward over the hook eye as it lies in the fly box. (We made this mistake once while tying several Pale Morning Sparkle Duns in a hurry one day. The next time we hit the Firehole, two days later, every one of the duns had the wing pointing in a forty-five degree angle forward over the hook eye. The fish did not mind but the flies were not as visible and they looked hideous.)

Next, tie in a section of sparkle poly for the shuck. The length of the shuck can vary from one-half to a full hook shank length. Most tiers tend to put on too heavy a shuck. Note the photograph. A new sparkle material called Z-lon is becoming a favorite shuck material of ours also. This comes in a thin single strand and is a little finer than sparkle poly. It works well on small (#18-#22) Sparkle Duns.

Finally, dub a fine, tapered body of the appropriate color, whip finish and go fishing.

Sparkle Dun

HOOK:	Mustad 94840 or equivalent; #16-#20 for Pale Morning Duns, #18-#22 for Tiny Western Olives, #16 for Mahogany Duns, #18-#22 for White Wing Blacks, #16 for Speckled Spinners, #14-#16 for Small Green Drakes, and #16-#18 for Blue Wing Olives.
THREAD:	6/0, color should match body color.
TAIL (SHUCK):	Sparkle poly or Z-lon. We like olive-brown for all western mayflies, length should be from one-half to a full hook shank.
BODY:	Natural or synthetic dubbings. We like rabbit or beaver fur. Pale Morning Dun: yellowish orange. Tiny Western Olive: grayish olive. Small Green Drake: dark olive. White Wing Black: black. Speckled Spinner: tan. Mahogany Dun: deep mahogany. Blue Wing Olive: dark olive.
WING:	Deer hair dyed dun is used for all Sparkle Duns except Speckled Spinners, for which we use natural mottled deer, and White Wing Blacks, for which we use white deer or antelope.

Sparkle Spinner

Vince Marinaro once wrote that he observed trout feeding exclusively on "fresh mayfly spinners". He went on to say that fresh spinners are those he thought were recognized by trout due to air bubbles trapped under the wings as they lay flush in the surface film. With this idea (and our Sparkle Dun) in mind we began using sparkle poly not only for the shuck on our Sparkle Duns but also for the wings on our spinner patterns.

The sparkle-poly-winged spinners outfish standard poly wings in nearly all instances. The wing has more "body" to it and resists collapsing and folding back along the body as a standard poly wing will do.

Whether it be for fishing the Pale Morning Dun spinner falls on the Henry's Fork, Firehole and spring creeks, the oversized Gray Drake spinners on Slough Creek, or the *Callibaetis* spinners during gulper time on Hebgen Lake, the Sparkle Spinners now occupy permanent places in our fly boxes.

The Sparkle Spinner is a simple fly to tie. Start the tying by attaching a half dozen or so tail fibers. Dub a thin body up to the wing position, about one-third of a hook shank back from the eye.

Next, using figure-eight wraps, tie on the sparkle poly wings. For this pattern less is best when it comes to wings. We have found that a sparse wing will always outfish a heavily tied wing. Most commercial flies of this type are tied with two to three times too much wing material. A small clump produces the desired sparkle effect — too much obscures the silhouette, and renders the fly less effective. Trim each wing to approximately the length of the hook shank.

Finish the fly by dubbing around the wings and up to the eye of the hook.

One more tip: many fly tiers will tie their spinners on extra light wire hooks. For Yellowstone area fishing use standard wire hooks or you will be straightened out many times.

Sparkle Spinner

HOOK:	Mustad 94840 or equivalent, #12-#20.
THREAD:	6/0 to match body color.
TAIL:	Dun hackle fibers or synthetic micro-fibbetts.
BODY:	Natural or synthetic dubbings. The important colors are rusty, tan, and olive.
WING:	White sparkle poly or white Z-lon.

Rusty Seal Spinner

One of the most valuable flies for fishing the Yellowstone area is also one of the least fished: the Rusty Spinner. With the prolific mayfly activity present here, it is surprising to us that many fishermen, even those with considerable experience in the area, seem to stop halfway in their fishing; they fish the emergence but ignore the inevitable fall of spinners. One law of physics says that for every action there is an equal and opposite reaction; the parallel fishing law says that for every mayfly hatch there is an opposite though, interestingly, not always equal spinner fall.

If we consider all the mayflies that are important to fishermen in this area, there is as much excellent spinner fishing as there is dun fishing. But when looked at individually we find species whose duns are more important than their spinners, species where dun and spinner importance is equal, and, appropriately enough, species whose spinners are considerably more important than their duns. For example, the Green Drakes are flies whose duns drastically outweigh spinners in significance; the Pale Morning Duns are mayflies with equally important duns and spinners; and the Gray Drake is a fly whose spinner fall is superb and emergence marginal.

Ask about the nature of the hatch you plan to fish: don't simply ask when the hatch starts and what fly you need to imitate the duns, ask if the spinners are important too, when they may fall, what size and color they are, is the spinner fall sporadic or concentrated. In effect, know the life history of the bug you are fishing. Natural flies are the root of this sport, and not to be familiar with them is, to us, unthinkable.

The seal spinner is one of our favorite imitations. It is

extremely translucent and well defined in the body, and has a very suggestive, translucent wing. Though we have illustrated the rusty version, keep in mind that this is as much a style of fly as it is a particular pattern. Tied fully spent, half spent, or with an upright wing for maximum visibility, it is an essential fly for the Yellowstone area.

Tying this fly is a bit tricky. Seal fur is a difficult material to dub, especially when tying small flies. For constructing the body, first choose what appears to be the correct amount of fur, keeping in mind it doesn't take much. Cut that amount in half. Cut it in half again. What's left should be just right. Dub the body. It should come out very sparse and very translucent.

The wing may be tied two ways. Natural seal can be clumped and tied on as would a piece of poly yarn; simply lay it across the hook and figure-eight it to the shank. This makes an unusual but effective wing. Our other choice of wing material is a synthetic called Magic Wing. Strands of this sparkly material are tied on figure eight style, then flared slightly to resemble a natural wing. This is accomplished by winding tying thread through the wing, causing the fibers to separate and stand out on their own.

Finish with a bit of rusty dubbing at the thorax and head.

Rusty Seal Spinner

HOOK:	Mustad 94840 or equivalent, #14-#20.
THREAD:	6/0 brown.
TAIL:	Dun hackle fibers.
BODY:	Rusty seal fur dubbing.
WING:	Natural seal fur or white Magic Wing.

Green Caddis Larva

On a comparative evolutionary scale, caddis of the genus *Rhyacophila* rank right in there with Cro-Magnon man. They are primitive.

In caddisfly evolution advancement is measured in part by the ability to build a protective case. *Rhyacophila* species lack this ability; they range freely over the bottom of riffles without the elaborate stick and stone cases exhibited by their relatives. Various species in this area are a bright, intense green; the color that has become well-known as "caddis green". This color has definitely not escaped the trout's notice, just as it should not escape the fisherman's.

Primitive caddisflies also need cold, highly oxygenated water, something pocket-water rivers like the Madison and Gallatin have an excellent supply of. It's no surprise that these rivers and others in the area hold tremendous populations of these caddis and that trout feed readily upon them as well. Since they do roam freely over the bottom of riffles, *Rhyacophila* larva are regularly dislodged by the current and occur often in the drift of a stream.

This may help explain why any number of popular green nymph patterns work so well in this area, and also why it is unwise to fish here without a few in your box. We fish our imitations on the bottom where the trout are accustomed to seeing the naturals, weighting the flies moderately and then adding split shot to the leader if necessary. Natural *Rhyacophila* are not capable of swimming or any other active means of rescuing themselves from the current, so our presentations are upstream, dead drift. A strike indicator on the leader will definitely aid in strike detection, as will fishing a short line.

Our *Rhyacophila* imitation is easy to tie. First weight the hook shank moderately. Dub a body of caddis green dubbing. The green we favor is an intense, chromatic green like the one naturals exhibit. It is a difficult color to come up with. Green seal fur looks the best because of its translucency (again like the naturals), but rabbit or Australian oppossum both work well too. After the body, take one or two wraps of starling hackle to suggest legs. Finish with a small black dubbed head. Whip finish.

Green Caddis Larva

HOOK: Mustad 9671 or equivalent, #12-#18, weighted.
THREAD: 6/0 black.
BODY: Caddis green dubbing.
HACKLE: Starling, one or two turns.
HEAD: Black dubbing.

Peeking Caddis Larva

Simply deadly! This pattern, a fly for all seasons, has been around for years but was ignored by most area fly fishermen until Bill Matthews of Jackson, Wyoming asked us to tie him a supply. Bill told us that this fly, in sizes #12 to #14, was the most consistent producer during his several consecutive weekends fishing the Slide Inn area of the Madison. We tied Bill his flies and a few for ourselves, using them later with great success.

Most commercial ties of this pattern use a drab olive for the "peeking" portion of the pattern. We have found that bright green and even a chartreuse dubbing produces noticeably better than the standard drab commercial ties. We fish the Peeking mostly in the pocket-water of the Madison and Gallatin, and quite possibly the bright or chartreuse green are more visible to the fish.

We fished the Peeking on December 6th this past season and had a day not soon to be forgotten. It had warmed up to 37 degrees on an overcast Saturday afternoon at the Grizzly Bar stretch of the Madison. We had been duck and goose hunting and having had some good shooting in the morning we decided to try the fishing in the early afternoon. Fishing up from the West Fork to the Grizzly Bar we located some really nice browns and rainbows in a feeding mood. An eighteen-inch hen rainbow that came out of the water three times within view of the highway brought a carload of cross-country skiers from Wisconsin to a stop. Down the bank they came and even though they were in training for several X-C races they had their fly fishing gear along so we gave them each a couple of Peeking Caddis to try. We expect a report on their success when they come back to Yellowstone country next March for our big ski race.

Some versions of the Peeking use tinsel chenille as an underbody with hare's ear loosely dubbed as an overbody. The tinsel chenille then peeks out from under the dubbing. While this seems to work on occasion our experience has shown that it is time consuming and unnecessary. A simple dubbed hare's mask body with a bright green dubbed larval section peeking out has been the most productive for us.

Begin the tying by wrapping the hook shank with lead wire. Using hare's mask, dub the abdomen two thirds of the way up the hook shank. Then dub the bright green peeking portion of the fly. Next tie in and take two wraps of a small brown partridge feather. Finish the fly with a small dubbed head and a whip finish.

Peeking Caddis Larva

HOOK:	Mustad 3906 or equivalent, #10-#14.
THREAD:	6/0 black.
BODY:	Roughly dubbed hare's mask.
PEEKING PORTION:	Bright green or chartreuse dubbing about

HACKLE: 1/4 the length of the entire fly.
           Brown Hungarian partridge.
HEAD: Black dubbing.

R.A.M. Caddis

Our good friend *Ross A. Merigold* (R.A.M.) developed this important Yellowstone area fly pattern. We have watched Ross fish it at the Slide Inn area of the Madison with great results. Although this pattern closely resembles a free-living caddis larva we feel it may also double as a cranefly larva. The Madison is packed with olive craneflies from Earthquake Lake to Ennis.

Ross tells us he prefers to fish it directly upstream, dead-drift using a strike indicator of bright poly yarn or brightly painted small cork. He maintains that these indicators offer great assistance in observing the take and controlling the depth of the nymph. Ross prefers to fish the RAM on or very near the bottom. He also says long casts are not necessary—twenty-five feet, including the leader, is maximum. A leader of 9 to 12 feet is preferred with a tippet seldom larger than 4x or 5x.

Ross likes to fish the RAM during caddis hatches or just before, fishing it as an emerger. He will also fish lakes with the RAM, on the bottom with a very, very slow hand-twist retrieve.

The RAM Caddis is most commonly tied and fished in sizes #10 and #12, however we have had great success at times with the RAM tied as small as #18. Most common colors include dark and light olive, brown, pink and orange. We have also used peacock and dubbed fur bodies.

Whether you use a body of floss, yarn, dubbing or herl

this pattern is deadly. We find it much easier to work with floss if we wet it prior to tying it in and wrapping the body. Floss is much more manageable when wet; it will not slip and slide down the hook nor will it separate and fray as easily. We sometimes use dubbing for the head (Ross builds up a large head of tying thread, then coats the head with multiple coats of thickened head cement).

In another slight but very effective variation, we tie the RAM as an emerger for caddis emergence situations. We then omit the lead and put a spun deer head clipped short. With the emerging RAM we have had some twenty-plus fish evenings presenting upstream dead drift or swinging and lifting the fly on a downstream float in front of feeding fish.

The RAM caddis is simple to tie. First tie in the gold rib at the rear of the hook. Then wind a body of floss over a lead wire underbody. The body should end two thirds of the way up the hook shank. Wrap a turn or two of white hen hackle where the body ends. Finally build a large head of tying thread or dubbing, and whip finish.

R.A.M. Caddis

HOOK:	Mustad 7957B, 94840 (for emerger) or equivalent, #10-#18.
THREAD:	6/0 claret, black or olive.
BODY:	Floss (light olive most common), yarn, peacock, or fur dubbing over lead wire.
RIB:	Gold wire. (Omit for emerger).
HACKLE:	White hen hackle.
HEAD:	Build up a large head of thread and coat with pre-thickened cement or just dub a head of dark brown fur. For the emerger style omit thread head and spin deer hair, clipping it short. Also omit lead wire underbody.

LaFontaine Sparkle Pupa

If there is a Yellowstone miracle fly not only for when caddis are emerging but also for searching the water this is it. When fish are on emerging caddis there is no better pattern than LaFontaine's Emergent Sparkle Pupa.

In our experience exact color is not that important most of the time. However, color contrast is. If the hatching caddis are light tan in color then a light colored antron bodied fly works better than a dark gray or olive. Of course it is far better to use the proper color if it can be obtained. But trying to imitate every color and size caddis one may come across in Yellowstone country would be quite a task. We tie these pupa in the following colors: dark gray and olive for the dark shades and caddis green and tan for the light shades. And since most rivers in the Yellowstone area are caddis rivers fly fishermen should have several of both the deep and emergent pupa in light and dark shades, sizes #12 to #18.

We cannot begin to say how many sparkle pupa we have given away to skeptics who doubt their effectiveness. Many of these skeptics had tried the grossly over-dressed commercial ties so often seen in fly bins across the country. Gary LaFontaine explains that the biggest problem he sees with commercial ties of his patterns is that they are almost always overdressed. Gary says that the sparser the tie the more effective it is.

A favorite technique in fishing the sparkle pupa is to locate a fish holding in the current during a non-hatch period. You can expect a rise by casting a Sparkle Pupa three to six feet above the fish and allowing it to pass within a foot of him. On more than one occasion we have watched our wildlife-artist friend Kevin Westlund take over a dozen twelve to twenty-inch browns and rainbows fishing this method on the Madison during August.

There have been times on the Henry's Fork and the Firehole during mayfly hatches when fish are really on the emerging duns. Just for fun we have cast to these rising trout Emergent Sparkle Pupa and have done very well, seeing fish move as much as three feet to intercept the pupa. At times it seems trout cannot refuse caddis pupa no matter what hatch they are working.

Of course fishing sparkle pupa prior to and during a caddis emergence provides great sport. Again, matching exact color generally is not crucial for success, but the angler should have patterns of the right size and approximate color shades. For instance, if the hatching caddis is a *Hydropsyche* which is very light tan in color and about a size #16, the fly fisherman will do very well using a #16 tan, gold or even light green pupa. We prefer fishing our pupa, both deep and emergent, upstream dead drift unless we are working caddis on the Henry's Fork, Firehole or the slick waters on the upper Yellowstone, where we then use the quartering downstream, slack line approach to individual feeding fish.

Sparseness is the key in tying successful Sparkle Caddis Pupa. Antron yarn is generally four stranded, and for sizes #12 to #16 we use two of the four strands. One strand is used on a size #18. If all four strands are used the fly is too bulky and noticeably less effective.

Start by tying in the strands of yarn used for the overbody at the bend of the hook. When tying in these strands push and force the fibers around the hook shank with pressure from a thumbnail. Next dub the sparsest body possible of antron yarn two thirds up the hook shank. Now bring the sparkle yarn strands forward and tie them down with a couple loose wraps of thread. With a bodkin pull the sparkle yarn away from the body to form a bubble-like overbody. Now lock the ends down with a few more firm wraps of nylon. Apply legs or wing depending on whether tying the deep or emergent pattern, dub a fur head and whip finish.

LaFontaine Sparkle Pupa

HOOK: Mustad 94840 or equivalent, #12-#18.

THREAD: 6/0 to match body color.

OVERBODY: Antron sparkle yarn encompassing hook shank and underbody in a distinct bubble. Our favorite colors and sizes are dark gray #14-#18, light green #14-#16, olive #14-#18, and tan #14-#16.

UNDERBODY: Antron yarn, very sparsely dubbed.

LEGS OR WING: Partridge or speckled hen back for legs on deep patterns; deer hair for wing on emergent patterns.

HEAD: Dubbed fur; dark brown Australian opossum for dark patterns and hare's mask dubbing for the lighter shades.

Paul's Caddis

Despite being a relatively new fly, this caddis has made a rapid ascent to popularity in our area, especially among the local "caddis cogniscenti."

It was first shown to us by Paul Brown, formerly a West Yellowstone school teacher and now a rod design consultant for the Fenwick Rod Company. Paul is a master on the Henry's Fork.

His caddis features a very realistic, well defined synthetic wing and a roughly dubbed body and head. The value of this is obvious: it can be fished as an emerger, an adult, or an egg-laying adult as the need arises. There is enough concreteness in its outline to represent unmistakably a caddis, yet at the same time it is vague enough to viably imitate any of these three stages. Its effectiveness is especially noticeable in flat water conditions, but is by no means limited to such situations. We have found this caddis as impressive on the turbulent Madison pocket water as it has been on the flats of the Henry's Fork. We usually dress it with floatant and fish it dry, just on or within the surface film.

The synthetic wing material (marketed by several companies) is a tightly woven, almost indestructible material very similar to that used by silkscreen printers. It is opaque, much like a natural caddis wing, and can be dyed different colors without losing the opacity.

This pattern is basically easy to tie, but there are a couple of important points worth noting. The wing does not provide much flotation so it is critical that the dubbing be very rough. Besides floating the fly, the dubbing gives an impressionistic feel that we think adds to its effectiveness. It will also take a time or two to get the wing lying correctly—low over the body and extending down over the sides of the fly.

To begin with, we prefer a rather coarse fur such as hare's ear, Australian opossum, or antron dubbing, all dyed to the appropriate shade. This is dubbed loosely right on the tying thread (or put in a dubbing loop) and wound on as a body. The desired effect is, again, a rough body. The wing is tied as follows. Cut a narrow strip of material and fold it in half lengthwise. The initial width will vary according to the size of hook. Experiment on your first few. Then tie in ahead of the body, leaving room for a fuzzy head. Trim the top angle of the wing first, then the bottom, as in the photograph. Finish with a roughly dubbed head.

Paul's Caddis

HOOK:	Mustad 94840 or equivalent, #14-#20.
THREAD:	6/0, color to match body.
BODY:	Roughly dubbed hare's ear, Australian opossum, or antron.
WING:	Synthetic wing material, trimmed.
HEAD:	Same dubbing as body, roughly dubbed or picked out.

Antron Caddis

If you ever judged a fly by simplicity of design alone, this caddis would have a good jump on the rest of the field. In fact, so simple is the design that it often belies the effectiveness of the pattern. Convincing people of its merit is often a difficult task; there just isn't a whole lot to the fly.

Look more closely at the ingredients though, and you can see why it is such a versatile and effective representation of a natural caddis. An antron body, to simulate any stage of caddisfly body, a flared deer hair wing, which can variously be interpreted as the wing of an emerging, fluttering, drowned, or egglaying adult, and finally the shaggy, suggestive dubbed head that enhances any of the above images.

The Henry's Fork was the testpiece for this fly, and the wild rainbows that see a steady stream of natural caddis during June and July accepted it eagerly. They took it during emergence, during egglaying periods, and in the afternoons when there was no caddis activity apparent at all. It floats low like a natural, yet the deer hair wing allows it to be skated along the surface if need be to imitate the skittering species of natural caddis.

Though used primarily as a smooth water fly, the Antron caddis is effective in rougher water too. It is harder to follow with the eye, but floats very well and fast-water fish will take it without hesitation. In pocket-water fishing during a caddis emergence or egglaying flight, we try to get as close to the fish as possible from immediately below him, often no more than ten or fifteen feet. This helps in casting accuracy, in seeing the fly, and allows greater control of slack line, always a problem in fast water. Quick, accurate, repetitive casting is often necessary, especially if the fish are seeing a lot of naturals coming their way. We always try to be careful though; even fast-water fish are put down by a sloppy cast banging the water.

Tying the Antron caddis is relatively easy. Selection of the proper deer hair is not and that is the most important step. Depending on the size of the fly, we look for straight, fine hair that has short tips and is hollow all the way down into the tips. If the hair is not hollow, the wing will not flare properly and the fly won't float well. Squeeze any prospective hair between thumbnail and forefinger. If you can feel it compress, if you can feel the hollowness and see it flare a bit, it's probably a good piece. If it just lies there or feels solid to the fingers, avoid it. Try this many times with different pieces of hair to see the wide variation that exists among natural deer.

With the right deer in hand, dub a rough body of antron about two-thirds up the hook shank. Stack the deer hair, amount to be determined by the size of fly and personal preference, and tie it in ahead of the body. It should flare out over the top 180 degrees (at least) of the hook and extend just beyond the bend. Dub a rough head to cover the remainder of the hook, being careful to not compress or condense the wing. Whip finish.

Antron Caddis

HOOK:	Mustad 94840 or equivalent, #14-#20.
THREAD:	6/0, olive or brown.
BODY:	Antron dubbing, green, black, olive, gold.
WING:	Deer hair, light or dark.
HEAD:	Rough dubbed of hare's ear or Australian opossum in tan or brown.

Fluttering Caddis

This is one of those old patterns whose effectiveness can never be denied. Even under demanding spring creek situations this fly comes through. It can be used to imitate not only caddisflies but stoneflies, grass and leaf hoppers, beetles, crickets, spruce moths and many more insects.

The Fluttering Caddis offers a different profile that fish seem to respond to when other popular patterns aren't working. The Elk Hair Caddis, for instance, has a palmered hackle which gives the impression of a skittering caddis on the surface. The Fluttering Caddis has a face hackle which means the body will be mostly on or in the surface film. At times on flat water or over a fish that refuses our fly we will even trim a notch in the bottom of the hackle, making the fly sit lower in the film. This has fooled the most difficult trout for us.

There are wonderful Little Yellow Stonefly hatches on our area rivers and streams each July and August. The Yellow Fluttering Caddis is a great representation of this hatch, besides working as a caddis imitation. Sort of "killing two hatches with one fly".

We once watched Nick Lyons use a #14 Yellow Fluttering Caddis to take a grand old brown trout below Varney Bridge on the Madison one hot, sunny August morning. There were a few caddis around that morning but they were the black micro-caddis, sizes #20-#22. There were a fair number of the Little Yellow Stones on the water and since Madison trout relish these during their morning egglaying flights in July and August, Nick tied on an imitation. Nick's son Tony decided on a Royal Wulff as we drifted under the bridge. Round the first bend, the current ripped hard into an undercut bank on the west side of the river. The yellowing leaves of wild rose bushes brushed the emerald waters of the river. Tony and I were talking about the area's wildlife when a big trout came up to pick off a natural several yards below. I said nothing of the fish to Nick, as his pattern was dancing along the edge of the undercut on a direct course with the trout. As we came up even with the fish's lie all three of us saw the big snout pierce the surface and take Nick's fly. The hook-jawed male's first leap came beneath the undercut; we heard his jump as a "thud-thud" from under the bank. Nick coaxed him out into the open river and upstream the fish ran, jumping and heading towards the boat. We bailed out at the next gravel bar, Tony with the net in hand. Another jump, a few more short runs and Tony skillfully netted the bronze beauty. After resting the fish and taking a few photographs he was released, the beginning of a day filled with many more fish coming to the Yellow Fluttering Caddis. It is a favorite pattern of Nick's and an important fly to have during July and August in Yellowstone country.

When tying this pattern look for elk hair that is fairly coarse and hollow. Fine elk hair is usually not hollow and will not flare to form the wing properly. Then too, hair that is too fine sinks like a rock.

To start the tying of any of the Fluttering Caddis, dub a body two-thirds the length of the hook shank. Stack a clump of elk hair to even the tips, and tie in downwing style where the body ends. The wing should extend just past the hook bend. Finally tie in and wind an appropriate size hackle. Whip finish to complete the fly.

We tie the fluttering caddis in many different color combinations. Our favorites are (listed as body color/wing color/hackle color: bright green/gray/grizzly, yellow/yellow/grizzly, dun/dun/dun, black/black/black, tan/natural/brown.

Fluttering Caddis

HOOK: Mustad 94840 or equivalent, #12-#20.
THREAD: 6/0 to match body color.

BODY:	Natural fur dubbing.
WING:	Natural or dyed elk hair.
HACKLE:	Grizzly, dun, black, or brown.

Elk Hair Caddis

Al Troth's Elk Hair Caddis is one of the most important patterns fly fishermen should have in their fly boxes for Yellowstone area fishing. This fly imitates the *Hydropsyche* caddis hatch on the Madison effectively and can be used for many other species as well. It is one of the standard Yellowstone caddis patterns.

For the fly tier the Elk Hair Caddis is one of the easiest patterns to master provided he has the right elk hair; not any piece will do. The tier should look for hair that is hollow well up into the tips—particularly for smaller sizes, #16 to #20. It is very important that the wing flare when tied in, to cup the top of the body in 180-degree fashion.

Selecting elk hair that is hollow into the tips is rather simple: search for a piece with short black tips and when thumb nail pressure is applied it should easily flare and compress. You do not necessarily want fine hair, which is generally not hollow and will not compress when tied in. Coarser hair is hollow and as a rule compresses and flares much better than fine hair.

Most fly tiers use too much wing of the wrong type or texture of hair. As a result the fly's wing is too bulky and does not flare or cup the body properly. The wing also tends to be unstable and spins freely on the hook shank. After a fish or two the wing often begins to pull out and fall apart.

Never use Monocord when tying the Elk Hair Caddis. If the elk hair will not flare using standard 6/0 nylon then the hair is not the proper type for the size fly being attempted. Monocord just adds more weight and bulk.

Generally we prefer this pattern with a light elk wing, but there are times when a natural dark elk wing or dyed elk wing can be most effective.

To tie the Elk Hair Caddis, begin by tying in the hackle at the rear of the hook. Dub a body of the desired color to just behind the hook eye. Palmer the hackle forward in even turns and tie off where the body ends. Trim the top of the hackle flat; this allows the wing to ride low over the body. After selecting and stacking the elk hair for the wing, tie it in with the tips extending just beyond the hook bend. Use six or seven tight turns of tying thread to anchor the wing to the hook. Pull the wing butts up and whip finish in *front* of the wing; this helps stabilize and secure the wing.

Elk Hair Caddis

HOOK: Mustad 94840 or equivalent, #10-#22.
THREAD: 6/0 olive, brown, or gray.
BODY: Olive, brown, or gray dubbing.
HACKLE: Brown or grizzly palmered.
WING: Elk hair; try some with light elk and some with dark elk. Most caddis have dark wings.

G and H Sedge

The G and H Sedge, or Goddard caddis as it is known around here, was invented by the Englishmen John Goddard and Cliff Henry. The pattern was originally tied as a lake fly and incorporated deer hair as a main ingredient to add what the two men felt were essential features for a satisfactory pattern: a lifelike silhouette, and the ability to float for long periods of time.

It is an excellent lake fly in Yellowstone country too; the clipped deer hair body effectively imitates the long-horn *Oecetis* caddis and other species that are active during the summer evenings. The naturals skitter and hop around on the surface, and the Goddard imitation can duplicate these motions while still floating well. Lake fishing during evening hours is not a very popular form of fishing out here, in part because of the unpredictability of the wind. When it blows, fishing is generally off. As a rule however, it stops blowing early enough in the evenings during the summer to allow a couple of hours of good fishing. Caddis are often the predominant insect.

As good a lake fly as it is, the main reason for the Goddard's popularity is the success it has on area rivers. Like other attractors, this fly floats well on rough water and is easy for the angler to see. But it has an advantage other attractors don't in that it presents a very realistic silhouette; it actually looks like a caddis. It can be used to attract and imitate at the same time. This pattern works as often on smooth waters like the Henry's Fork as it does on rough and tumble freestoners like the Gallatin.

The Goddard caddis is not an easy fly to tie, though with the proper materials it presents less of a challenge than many tiers suspect. Good spinning deer hair that is also quite fine is the essential ingredient. Have someone with a solid knowledge of deer hair select some appropriate pieces. Begin by spinning the body; this should be accomplished with two clumps of hair, no more or less, regardless of the size of fly. The first clump is attached and spun where a conventional tail would be tied in—just ahead of the bend. The second clump should be packed right against the first, and should end with the front half of the hook shank showing. This may seem like too short a body, but once it's trimmed it will be perfect. Not leaving adequate room for the hackle is a common error that results in a misproportioned fly.

MAYFLIES

Pheasant Tail Nymph

Fur Nymph

Peacock

Green Drake Emerger

Green Drake Paradrake

Sparkle Dun

Sparkle Spinner

Rusty Seal Spinner

CADDISFLIES

Green Caddis Larva

Peeking Caddis Larva

R.A.M. Caddis

LaFontaine Sparkle Pupa

CADDISFLIES

Paul's Caddis

Antron Caddis

Fluttering Caddis

Elk Hair Caddis

G and H Sedge

STONEFLIES

Nature Stonefly Nymph
Mature

Nature Stonefly Nymph
Black Willow

Nature Stonefly Nymph
Amber

Brook's Stonefly Nymphs

Matt's Adult Stone

Little Yellow and
Olive Stoneflies

TERRESTRIALS

Blue Ribbon Foam Beetle

Flying Ant

Madison River Stopper

Jay-Dave's Hopper

GENERAL DRY FLIES

Adams

Royal Wulff

Horner Deer Hair

H and L Variant

Griffith's Gnat

NYMPHS

*Giant and Summer
Crane Fly Larvae*

Prince Nymph

Zug Bug

Feather Duster

Hare's Ear

Soft Hackles

Midge Pupa

Yellowstone Scud

STREAMERS

Woolhead Sculpin

Soft Hackle Streamer

Wooly Bugger

Leech

Trim the body to a caddis shape, as in the photographs, before continuing. Then tie in two stripped hackle stems for antennae. Finally, tie in and wrap two brown hackles ahead of the body, finishing with a whip finish.

G and H Sedge

HOOK: Mustad 94840 or equivalent, #12-#18.
THREAD: For #12, 3/0 brown Monocord.
             For #14-#18 6/0 brown.
BODY: Deer hair, spun and clipped.
HACKLE: Brown.
ANTENNAE: Stripped brown hackle stems.

Nature Stonefly Nymphs
(Mature, Black Willow, and Amber)

When most fly tiers look at these nymphs they usually reply "too complicated, pretty to look at but I'll bet they're not worth the time and effort to tie". Well, from many years experience with this pattern we know it is worth your tying time and efforts. The fly is not hard to master but it does take time and when the tier gets to where he is finishing one every ten minutes he should think of turning professional.

As the name suggests, the "Mature Stone" represents the mature *Pteronarcys californica* (Giant Black

Stone) just prior to its emergence. At this time the natural's belly may turn from a dirty orange to a brilliant fire orange in color. Trout seem to key on this orange to the point that we now always incorporate an exaggerated fluorescent orange belly on our imitations. There is no doubt that this flash of orange makes a big difference in this fly's effectiveness.

Begin the Mature Stone by tying in the stripped goose tails. Weight the front half of the hook with lead wire. Attach the swannundaze rib, and yarn for the underbody. Wrap the yarn underbody to the hook eye and then back over the thorax. Tie off and cut the excess yarn. Advance the thread to the rear of the hook and tie in the orange belly material. Dub forward one-half of the hook shank with the black dubbing. Pull the belly yarn under the abdomen and secure. Rib the abdomen with even wraps of swannundaze, and tie it off.

Perhaps the largest stumbling block in tying these nymphs is the wing cases. Trim the wing cases from latex sheets, using the photographs as a guide. Make sure a long front end is left, for ease of handling and for forming the head. The first wing case is seated about one-half the way up the hook shank, after a soft pad of dubbing is wrapped on the yarn underbody. If this portion is dubbed too tightly the latex wingcase will buckle and fold in undesireable configurations. Trim the butt end of the first wing case.

Now dub forward a small amount of fur in preparation for seating the second wing case. Again, as with the rear wing case a soft pad of dubbing must be prepared for the front case to seat into. Secure the front case with 2 to 3 wraps of thread. Do not trim off the front tag of this wing case. At this point tie in the leg material, and dub to the hook eye. Wrap the thread back to the legs. Make one turn of hackle and tie off. Advance the thread halfway to the hook eye. Fold the latex tag forward and secure with 2 to 3 wraps of thread. Do not trim the remaining latex. At this point dub to the hook eye again. Pull latex over the last dubbed section and secure at hook eye. Trim latex off (finally!), and tie in two goose quills for antennae.

Whip finish and head cement.

All three of these patterns are tied in the same manner but the materials obviously change.

During the winter months we enjoy heading down to Varney Bridge and fishing downstream a mile or two. The Black Willow Nymph, in sizes #6 and #8, is the only nymph one needs to have a banner day. Some of the rainbows up from Ennis Lake and the Channels to spawn in this stretch have reached miniature steelhead proportions.

As with the Brook's Yellow Stone Nymph, at times the fish are on lighter shades of stonefly nymphs and show a definite preference for our Amber Stone. Particularly in waters where rainbows and cutthroats are found, Amber Stones can be very effective.

Nature Stonefly Nymphs
Mature Stone

HOOK:	Mustad 37160, #2-#4.
THREAD:	3/0 black Monocord.
TAILS:	Brown or amber dyed goose quills.
RIB:	#21 or #18 Swannundaze.
BELLY:	Fluorescent orange yarn.
ABDOMEN:	Black wool underbody, overwrapped with rough dubbed body of black Australian opossum and rabbit with spikey guard hairs left in.
WING CASE:	Pronotum, and Head: dyed latex cut to shape.
LEGS:	Pheasant back feather wound one turn over thorax.
THORAX:	Same as abdomen, over a lead wire foundation.
ANTENNAE:	Dyed brown or amber quoose quills.

Black Willow Stone

HOOK:	Mustad 37160, #4-#8.
THREAD:	3/0 orange Monocord.
TAILS:	Brown dyed goose quills.
RIB:	#18 Swannundaze and fine oval silver tinsel (optional).

ABDOMEN: An underbody of black wool yarn dubbed over with a rough body of black Australian opossum with spikey guard hairs left in.

WING CASE: Pronotum, and Head: Brown dyed latex cut to shape.

LEGS: Mottled pheasant neck or back feather.

THORAX: Orangish yellow dubbing, over a foundation of lead wire. We prefer natural fur with spikey guard hairs left in.

ANTENNAE: Brown dyed goose quills.

Amber Stone

HOOK: Mustad 37160, #4-#8.

THREAD: 3/0 orange Monocord.

TAILS: Brown dyed goose quills.

RIB: Brown polyester sewing thread.

UNDER-
BODY: Amber wool yarn.

OVERBODY: #17 Swannundaze.

WING CASE: Pronotum, and Head: Brown dyed latex cut to shape.

LEGS: Natural brown mottled pheasant back or neck feather.

THORAX: Amber natural dubbing.

ANTENNAE: Brown dyed goose quills.

Brook's Stonefly Nymphs

For a big ugly stonefly nymph these patterns are tough to beat. Charlie used to look at our own Nature Stonefly Nymphs and say, "These ain't ugly enough!".

Charlie believed that these large nymphs should be tied "in the round", that is, with no top or bottom to the fly or wing cases. He felt that flies tied this way were just as effective as the more complicated ties. His stonefly nymphs are simple to tie, durable, and indeed effective.

The first time we ever fished the Brooks Montana Stone was on the Gardner River upstream from its junction with the Yellowstone. It was a very snowy, calm day in late October. You could actually hear it snow; flakes the size of fifty cent pieces were coming down so hard it made following the strike indicator a difficult task.

Making short casts of fifteen feet and less we worked our way upstream all the way to the hot pots above the 45th parallel bridge in Yellowstone Park. The fish were in a taking mood, and the action was steady all afternoon. The real frosting on the cake, however, was Craig's almost hooking one of two women "hotpotters" he did not notice due to the snow and steam coming off the hot spring where it fed the Gardner. We never were sure who was more surprised and embarrassed as the gals ran to their stash of clothes and we exited downstream.

That day Charlie's Montana Stone made a believer of us. For pocket water this pattern is very killing, particularly in the early (May to June) and late seasons (September to November).

Charlie's Yellow Stone Nymph is a very good representation of the large golden stone nymphs of the Yellowstone area. There are times when the black stone nymphs just do not produce as well as the Yellow Stone Nymphs and at these times the lighter colored nymphs are a valuable pattern to have in the fly boxes. Rainbows and cutthroat seem to relish the Yellow Stone Nymph, so when fishing the upper Yellowstone, Box Canyon of the Henry's Fork and Gallatin always have them along.

After weighting the hook shank and tying in the tails, attach the wire rib and black wool yarn. Wind the wool yarn forward to form the abdomen and rib with the copper wire. Tie in the hackles and ostrich gills at the thorax position. Form a thorax with wool yarn wraps and tie off the excess. Wrap two turns of each hackle, side by side, and tie them off. Wind the ostrich gills, closely following the turns of hackles, and tie off. Finish with a whip finish.

Brook's Stonefly Nymphs
Montana Stone (imitates *Pteronarcys californica)*

HOOK:	Mustad 79580 or equivalent, #2-#8.
THREAD:	6/0 black.
TAIL:	Black stripped goose quills or crow primary fibers.
RIB:	Copper wire.
BODY:	Black wool yarn.
HACKLE:	One natural grizzly saddle and one grizzly dyed dark brown, two turns of each on the thorax.
GILLS:	White ostrich herl wrapped at the base of the hackles.

Yellow Stone (imitates *Hesperoperla pacifica* and *Calineuria californica).*

HOOK:	Mustad 79580 or equivalent, #4-#8.
THREAD:	6/0 yellow or tan.
TAIL:	Mottled cinnamon turkey primaries.
RIB:	Gold yarn and gold wire.
BODY:	Brown or brownish-tan yarn.
HACKLE:	Two turns each of natural and dyed brown grizzly saddle hackles.
GILLS:	Light grey ostrich herl wrapped at the base of each turn of hackle.

Matt's Adult Stone

This is an extremely effective pattern combining a body of woven poly macrame cord, wing of elk mane and collar and head of spun deer hair clipped to shape.

This fly produces browns and rainbows from the Madison and Yellowstone rivers to as far away as British Columbia's Dean and Bulkley River's, where it takes steelhead on the dry fly. It is durable; we have taken up to seventeen fish on one fly. Because of the poly and deer hair it floats like a cork and is really an easy fly to tie; what more could a fly tier ask for?

Not only do we use it in orange for the Salmonfly (*Pteronarcys californica*) hatch but we also tie it in gold and yellow for the Golden Stonefly (*Calineuria califonica*) and Willow Stonefly (*Hesperoperla pacifica*) hatches.

Tied properly, this pattern produces a very low riding fly. No hackle is used to obscure the silhouette. Granted, there are many times during the famed salmonfly hatches when the fish are on the skittering, egg laying adults, but there are also times when the high riding, bushy hackled patterns used to imitate that motion are refused; a realistic silhouette is needed. Another instance that calls for a low riding pattern is when red ants attack the naturals while they are at rest in the willows and chew their legs off. The naturals often end up falling on to the water and riding down the currents motionless. This fly is also good when the adults, weak from egglaying, fall spent to the surface. A low profile pattern like Matt's Stone is the answer.

While this pattern does not ride high on the water it can be made to skitter and burble in the riffles and rips because of its excellent floatability. We like to skitter and twitch it across and down when fish are taking naturals behaving similarly. Nothing is more explosive and exciting than a large trout taking naturals in this manner. This technique also works for dry fly steelhead when these monsters are on the October Caddis.

The first step in tying the Matt's Stonefly is to cut a section of poly cord about one to one and a half inches long. Burn one end of the cord to melt the fibers together. This prevents fraying. Then tie in the unburned end midway up the hook shank. Next tie in a wing of elk mane, extending just beyond the body. Dub a small amount of fur over the wing butts to cover the thread wraps; this makes for a neater looking fly when finished.

Then tie in two clumps of deer hair, one on either side, to represent kickers. Finally, spin a deer hair head and trim to shape.

Matt's Adult Stonefly

HOOK:	Mustad 94840 or equivalent, #4-#8.
THREAD:	3/0 Monocord, to match body color.
BODY:	Orange, gold or yellow poly macrame cord.
WING:	Elk mane.
KICKERS:	Deer hair.
HEAD:	Spun deer clipped to shape.

Little Yellow and Olive Stoneflies

A few hatches in Yellowstone country are overlooked by fishermen. Two of them are important stonefly emergences which provide some of the season's best dry fly fishing—if the fly fisherman has the right fly. Usually these insects come off on our warm, sunny July and August mornings or early afternoons. Most fly fishermen are then eating lunch, napping or tying flies in preparation for the evening caddis or mid-afternoon grasshopper activity and miss this emergence.

This is one of those hatches where the insects are seldom seen on the water. For most of their 10 to 20 day adult lives these bugs can be seen crawling on rocks, streamside vegetation, or on waders and fly vests. Really, the only times these diminutive Plecoptera are on the water are when they fall or are blown back on the water during their emergence, or when skittering on the surface expelling their egg masses.

Remember, the activity is seldom heavy and always short lived; it lasts only one to two hours daily. The fish will nonetheless key on these insects.

Naturals run in color from chartreuse to gold to olive. An extremely effective pattern for us uses a bright red tag of tying thread, dubbed gold body, fluorescent yellow dyed elk or deer wing and a hackle of grizzly or ginger. We would not be without several of these ties in our boxes as they provide wonderful action for six to eight weeks each summer.

We feel this fly may also be taken for some of the lighter colored caddis, spruce moths and even grasshoppers present during July and August.

There are many warm, sunny days on the Madison and Gallatin during which the Little Yellow or Olive Stonefly is the only fly we will fish. One such day was in mid-July when three of us took and released over 50 rainbows and browns on the Gallatin near Big Sky. None were over 17 inches but we had continuous action for two hours, from 10:00 A.M. to 12 noon, before a thunderstorm forced us to the truck for lunch and drying out.

Tying these stoneflies is easy. Begin by wrapping a short tag of red thread at the rear of the hook. Dub a body two thirds of the way up the hook shank. Tie in a down wing of elk hair that extends just past the hook bend. Look for hollow hair for winging this fly. This allows the tying thread to sink into and compress the hair, avoiding bulk at the tie in point. Hollow hair also flares well, making the fly float better and more visible to the angler.

The last step is to tie in and wrap the hackle at the front of the hook, tying off with a whip finish.

Little Yellow and Olive Stoneflies

HOOK: Mustad 94840 or equivalent, #14-#18.
THREAD: 6/0, red or olive.
TAG: Red tying thread.
BODY: Bright yellow or olive dubbing.
WING: Yellow or olive elk hair.
HACKLE: Grizzly or ginger.

Blue Ribbon Foam Beetle

The "fastest beetle in the west"—to tie! During the dog days of August when fishing is demanding on the Madison, Henry's Fork or spring creeks this fly will out-fish all others in non-hatch situations. During Diptera emergences in mid-winter this fly will take fish after fish, because it imitates a mating clump of midges.

Last August 28th there was no hopper wind, no caddis hatch, and not many clouds in the sky but we had a day off from work and were determined to have a good afternoon of fishing. Working up from Pine Butte in the catch and release section of the Madison we fished side by side and took over twenty nice browns and rainbows in the twelve to seventeen inch class—all on a #12 black Foam Beetle. We watched some fish travel over three feet and take the fly in a gentle sip.

If there is a drawback to any beetle pattern it is that they are hard flies to see. We do not know who first put a small clump of flourescent pink yarn on the top of beetle patterns several years back but it sure helps in tracking the fly. The yarn does not seem to hinder the fly's effectiveness and since we have natural beetles present in great numbers from June through September which have a brilliant pink to orange band at the head, the yarn can make the fly even that much more realistic.

We have referred to the black beetle but how about those metallic green Tiger beetles we all see streamside? We have tied and fished bright green foam beetles with equally good success, although we have not found an instance where the fish refused the black and took the green or vice versa.

The biggest attractions to this pattern are that it is easy to tie, unsinkable, and extremely durable. We use a closed cell foam called polycelon for the body. This material has proven far superior to any type of hair we have ever tried, and the use of elk hair for legs instead of deer hair also adds durability.

Cut a thin strip of foam a couple of inches long. Tie in the strip on top of the hook shank wrapping from hook eye back to bend. The foam will compress easily and should anchor securely to the hook. Select three coarse dyed black elk hair fibers and tie them on crosswise just behind the hook eye. The legs should stand out at ninety degrees from the hook shank. Fold the strip of foam over the top of the body in shellback fashion and tie down at the hook eye. Whip finish and trim the leftover foam, leaving a short head at the hook eye.

Blue Ribbon Foam Beetle

HOOK:	Mustad 94840 or equivalent, #12-#18.
THREAD:	6/0 black.
BODY:	Black polycelon tied on hook shank.
SHELLBACK:	Black polycelon folded forward over the top of the fly.
LEGS:	Dyed coarse black elk hair.
HEAD:	Trimmed end of polycelon.

Flying Ant

The flying ant is the kind of pattern you may reach for only a couple of times each summer, but when you need it nothing else will do. Precisely when and where flights of flying ants will show up is a true mystery; we only know that on certain streams they will make an appearance sometime during the summer. Slough Creek, the Lamar River, the Madison River, the Henry's Fork — these waters and more all have moments when the surface is covered with flying ants, and without an adequate imitation success is impossible.

We once faced such a situation on lower Slough Creek. It was around 3:30 P.M. on a day that had been far from productive. Late morning clouds kept the temperature down and the normally active hoppers were just not getting on the water. Fish were not in position along the banks, and even in the pools and backwaters there were few fish dimpling the surface.

On our way back downriver, just prior to leaving and relegating the day to the "could have been better" category, we did notice several fish beginning to work, and work rather steadily at that. We watched for a minute or two as more fish joined in. After a dismal day, this was just what we needed to see. A cursory inspection of the water revealed thousands of flying ants pinioned in the surface. Trout dearly relish ants, and will feed wantonly on them for as long as the current continues to serve them. Knowing it was flying ant season and being prepared allowed us to defend ourselves rather nicely; we fished size #20 imitations and landed several beautiful cutthroat and rainbows.

Having at least a few imitations of flying ants is an absolute necessity for the summer months of July, August, and early September. The stories are legion of anglers witnessing a great fall of ants and suffering the consequences of having no matching patterns; less frequent, unfortunately, are the tales of complete success had with the proper imitations.

The ant pattern we have come to favor is tied primarily with synthetics. Black polycelon (a closed cell foam) makes up the body, and the wing is tied out of Magic Wing—bright sparkly strands of synthetic material.

Begin by tying on a thin strip of polycelon at the rear of the hook, wrapping tightly to compress the material. Advance the thread one-third of the way up the hook shank and pull the polycelon over the top, tying it down to create the rear "gaster". Then tie on a dozen strands of Magic Wing, facing the rear, and split them evenly to the sides with tying thread. This represents the wings. Trim the strands to about the length of the hook shank. Follow with two or three turns of black hackle in front of the wing, trimmed on the bottom. Finish by creating another polycelon gaster at the front of the hook, and whip finish.

Flying Ant

HOOK:	Mustad 94840 or equivalent, #14-#20.
THREAD:	6/0 black.
BODY:	Black polycelon tied in two parts.
WING:	White Magic Wing, tied in strands.
HACKLE:	Black, two or three turns.

Madison River Stopper

Local guide Nick Nicklas presented this pattern to us several years ago during hopper season. Guiding occupies a large portion of his time in the summer, with little left over for tying, so Nick is always searching for simpler and quicker ways to imitate natural insects. This is his solution for an effective fast-water hopper pattern. It also doubles as an excellent golden stonefly imitation when stoneflies are in season.

At first glance, the design of the Stopper tends to make skeptics out of anglers accustomed to fishing realistic hopper patterns. From our experience, however, the features the Stopper possesses are all that are necessary to dupe hopper feeding trout in pocket-water situations. None of the more elaborate, realistic patterns have outfished this fly under these conditions.

Exactly what features a hopper pattern needs in order to provoke a strike from a trout are unknown. Even if, through further work, we can determine what is important (whether it be overall shape, size, legs, a prominent body, etc.), more and more we are beginning to believe that pattern may only be of secondary importance anyway.

Our current line of thought is that factors such as the time of year, angling pressure, angling methods, the particular river being fished, water level, species of trout, etc., exert as much influence on hopper feeding trout as does the size and pattern of fly being fished. Precisely what all the factors are and how they interact is still a subjective, nebulous array of ideas, and remains an open area to be worked upon.

It seems there will always be a need for a separate slow-water pattern (which will probably be more realistic) but until the important factors in imitating a hopper are ferreted out and defined (if that's possible), it doesn't appear necessary to use more complicated patterns in faster water.

The ease of tying the Stopper is one of its nicest features. Begin by cutting a thin strip of yellow polycelon and tying it on at the rear of the hook. Create an extended body by looping a short section of the polycelon and tying it down at the same point it was tied in at. This loop of polycelon should be quite short. Wrap the remaining strip of polycelon firmly but not tightly on the hook shank (you don't want to compress all the air from it) and tie off just behind the hook eye.

Tie in an underwing of golden pheasant tippet that extends just past the body in length. Over the underwing bind down a single clump of deer hair the same length as the underwing. The deer hair is not spun but is simply bound down on top of the shank. Pull the butts of the deer hair up, whip finish under them, and trim the butts short, as in the photograph.

Madison River Stopper

HOOK:	Mustad 94840 or equivalent, #10-#14.
THREAD:	3/0 Monocord, yellow.
BODY:	Yellow Polycelon.
UNDERWING:	Golden pheasant tippet strands.
WING:	A clump of whitetail deer.
HEAD:	Deer hair butts trimmed close.

Jay-Dave's Hopper

Named for its originators, Jay Buckner and Dave Whitlock, this pattern was introduced in 1978 in the *Second Fly Tyers Almanac.* It has become a standard grasshopper pattern in the Yellowstone area.

Yellowstone hopper season begins in mid-July and continues into October, sometimes as late as the third week. The first frosts of fall have little effect on these hardy insects. Even after the false-winter snowstorms of early October, hoppers can be observed clamoring about streamside vegetation as the sun returns to warm things up.

With the preponderance of grasshoppers in our area, it is only natural that there are many, many hopper imitations to choose from. It seems everybody who fishes this area has their own favorite. This pattern has always been one of our choices because it floats well but rides low in the water, and has a good, clean hopper silhouette. Controversy continues as to the need and effectiveness of legs on hopper imitations. We feel that for the majority of fishing situations legs are not necessary, consequently we tie this fly without legs as often as we include them. Legs may help in smooth, slow water conditions where trout get a long, leisurely look at the naturals and our imitations.

Overall size and silhouette seem to be the factors that influence success more than individual features such as legs. When we are getting refusals to our hoppers, changing to a smaller size is our first reaction. If this fails, we either trim the fly down to make it sparser, or drown the fly and fish it wet. Larger trout can often be taken by fishing a wet hopper pattern; sunken grasshoppers are nothing new to trout and perhaps taking the fly underwater allows the fish an extra feeling of security.

Begin tying this hopper by attaching a tail of red deer or hackle fibers to the hook. Follow that with a length of poly yarn and a brown hackle, both tied in at the rear of the hook. Wind the poly forward two-thirds the length of the shank. Pa. ᵧer the hackle to the same point and tie off. Trim the t of the hackle flush with the body. The sides and bottᴄ should be trimmed to just under a hook gap in lenᵧ

After treating a turkey quill with vinyl cement, cut a small section off the quill and tie it in to form the wing. Next tie in the two legs, one on either side of the wing. A deer hair collar should be tied on after the legs. Use one clump of hair and make it about one-half the length of the legs. The final step is to spin a deer hair head and trim it to shape.

Jay-Dave's Hopper

HOOK: Mustad 94831 or equivalent, #6-#12.
THREAD: 3/0 Monocord, tan or yellow.
TAIL: Red hackle fibers or deer hair.
BODY: Cream, yellow, green, or tan poly yarn, with a brown hackle palmered over the yarn.
WING: A section of a mottled turkey tail or wing quill, treated with vinyl cement.
COLLAR: Deer hair, extending one-half the length of the legs.
HEAD: Spun deer hair, clipped to shape.

Adams

If allowed but one dry fly, how many experts would choose the Adams? Maybe all of them. While there is no need to make it your sole choice for fishing around Yellowstone, the Adams is indisputably an extremely deadly fly and is certainly worth carrying in a range of sizes.

The Adams can suggest several mayfly species, caddis, midges, even some terrestrials, and do it very well. As an imitator it is equally valuable; consider this list of Yellowstone hatches an Adams can cover: In size #20, a better imitation of adult midges for many of our waters is hard to come by; a #18 and a #20 both imitate the prolific *Baetis* mayflies; a #16 works beautifully as a *Callibaetis* in standard, spentwing, or parachute styles; a #12 Adams nicely represents the *Siphlonurus* or Gray Drake mayflies; a #14 and #16 can suggest several fast water *Epeorus* mayflies, and the list goes on...

Brown trout are particularly fond of (or is it susceptible to?) the Adams. One of our favorite lines (and we issue this only half-jokingly) is that the brown hasn't been born that feeds on the surface and can refuse a #20 Adams. We have been in many situations where fish seemed anxious to demonstrate this fact to us. Several of the most pleasant were some early spring evenings spent on Nelson's Creek awhile back. The Diptera became active towards dark, coaxing the browns out from under the logs to begin their nightly meal. The delicate sipping rises were difficult to see until we had seen enough to really recognize them (a catch-22 situation), and even then one almost had to be looking in exactly the right spot. A #20 Adams carefully presented was deadly medicine and accounted for many nice fish.

The most popular spot for fishing the Adams is probably Hebgen Lake during the *Callibaetis* hatch. These speckled mayflies have daily emergences and spinner falls for almost two months during the summer, and an Adams is a worthy choice for both dun and spinner. Standard ties, spentwings, and parachutes all work well, though three different fishermen will give you three different answers as to which style is best. Even so, it is hard to go wrong with any of them.

Tying the standard Adams is a straightforward affair. Begin by tying on the wings, which should be made from grizzly hen hackle tips. After tying them in, they should be brought upright and divided at roughly a 45 degree angle with the tying thread. Tie on the tail next, making sure to maintain a smooth foundation for the body. Dub a thin body of muskrat, leaving ample room for the hackle. The grizzly and brown hackles are then tied in and wound. With two feathers to wind it is easy to overhackle a fly; two turns behind and in front of the wings with each hackle is sufficient. Whip finish to form a small, tight head.

Adams

HOOK: Mustad 94840 or equivalent, #12-#20.
THREAD: 6/0 gray.
TAIL: Mixed grizzly and brown hackle fibers.
BODY: Muskrat dubbing.
WING: Grizzly hen hackle tips.
HACKLE: Mixed brown and grizzly.

Royal Wulff

L.Q. Quackenbush. Now there is a hard-to-forget name that flyfishing history has not been particularly kind to. Though his name and place have been largely forgotten among anglers, L.Q. is the real inventor of the Royal Wulff, or, as it was called back then, the Quack Coachman. It was he who suggested to Rube Cross that white hair wings and a hair tail would make a more durable substitute for the feather wings and tail used on the Fan Wing Royal Coachman. Thus was born the first "Royal Wulff".

It was rechristened as a Wulff about the time Lee Wulff's hairwing series became popular. L.Q.'s name fell into oblivion but his fly has become a standard, particularly in the West.

Parentage aside, consider the aspects of the fly itself. The white hair wings, the hair tail, heavy brown hackle, a touch of the mystical peacock, and a hint of red floss. This combination has become the *tour de force* of western hairwings, easily one of the top selling and top producing flies in this region. The fly floats well in rough water, and is readily seen by both fish and fisherman. It catches fish after fish, and not just those from the pocket-water.

Many anglers count on this fly in sizes #16 and #18 as their secret weapon for "tough" rivers like the Henry's Fork. It is a capital brown trout fly and on the Firehole, for instance, it will make otherwise difficult fish ridiculously easy at times. We won't try to explain it, but the fly works when by all rights it shouldn't have a chance.

For a western float trip, the Royal Wulff is essential baggage. In sizes #8 to #12 it will pound up fish from the middle of the river; it suggests to a fish a meal worth travelling for. In the smaller sizes it is excellent along the edges, and many fishermen feel one of the reasons for this is that it imitates a flying ant; a common sight during the summer. It is certainly a possibility.

Tying the Royal Wulff calls for patience and a good eye for proportion. Note the wing position in this picture—not too far forward and not too far back. After tying the wing on, add a tail of moose hair. The butts of the tail should meet those of the wing, leaving no gaps or bumps that could ruin the body. Use two or three strands of peacock for the body; this adds fullness and also is more durable than a single strand. After forming the back third of the body do not cut the peacock off; simply tie it down along the hook shank until it reaches the point where the front section will begin. Wrap a smooth, thin band of red floss over the tied down peacock. Trim the floss and then wrap the remaining peacock to finish the body. Do not crowd the area where the hackle will go. Finish with two brown hackles and a small, tight head.

Royal Wulff

HOOK:	Mustad 94840 or equivalent, #8-#20.
THREAD:	6/0 black.
TAIL:	Moose body hair.
BODY:	Peacock herl, divided in the middle by a band of red floss.
WING:	White calf body hair.
HACKLE:	Brown.

Horner Deer Hair

Here is a pattern that most local fly fishermen would never be without. Our good friend Frank Matarelli tells us that Jack Horner of San Francisco came up with this gem many years ago. Patterns like the Goofus Bug, which was perfected by Pat and Zig Barnes, and the Humpy (another local favorite), are closely related to the Horner Deer Hair, standing as testaments to the effectiveness of this tried and true fly. The Gallatin, Madison, Yellowstone and Canyon stretches of the Henry's Fork are our favorite waters to fish with the Horner Deer Hair. If tied with the proper materials this fly is next to impossible to sink. This modern method of tying differs from Horner's original pattern which called for hackle of relatively poor quality and only 4 wraps of it. Horner maintained that not the hackle but the hair floated the fly, "on the water and not above it".

The "modern" heavily hackled Horner Deer Hair (Goofus Bug-Humpy) floats like a cork and is an easy fly to see on the water—a big plus when fishing the heavy pocket-water on some of Yellowstone country's swifter streams. Area guides like the yellow Horner Deer Hair in sizes #8-#14 fished in the heaviest riffles. It is especially effective during the grasshopper season.

The Horner Deer Hair is a difficult fly to tie, but using this method will help make it easier. First tie in a tail of elk or moose hair. Then tie in wings of elk, leaving long butt ends since these will be bound down from the wings back to the tail and forward again over the body to form the shell back. Pull the wings upright and with wraps of thread secure them in this position. Divide the wing equally with figure eight wraps. Bind down the trailing butts ends at the bend of the hook, covering them completely with the thread. Advance the thread to behind the wing, pull the butt ends over the top of the body and tie down to form the shellback. Trim any remaining butts.

Now tie in two hackles and wind them in back and in front of the wings. Finish with a whip finish.

Some of the old timers in this area still use Horner's method of applying the body. They simply crisscross the tying thread over the underbody of elk rather than overwrapping it to form a solid colored body of tying thread. Horner also preferred deer hair for wings and body of this fly, but we find elk to be more durable and available in a wider range of colors.

Horner Deer Hair

HOOK: Mustad 94840 or equivalent, #8-#18.
THREAD: 6/0 yellow, black, olive and red.

TAIL: Moose or elk hair.
WING: Elk hair upright and divided.
BODY: Formed from the butt ends of the wing.
HACKLE: The original pattern calls for two turns of
           low grade grizzly hackle in back of and
           two turns in front of the wings. Most ties
           today use a mixture of top quality grizzly
           and brown hackle tied heavy enough to
           keep the fly above the film, not in or on it.

H and L Variant

H and L, Ike's fly, and House and Lot. Regardless of its several monikers, this fly is as much a part of Yellowstone fishing as are steely-eyed guides rowing drift boats, from which, incidentally, thousands of these flies are cast every summer. This could possibly be one of those flies that catches so many fish only because so many fishermen use it.

As a fast water fly, however, there are those fishermen (and guides) who feel it is without peer. It floats well, suggests about anything that might be on the water, and can be seen not only by the fish but by fishermen. Visibility to the angler is an attribute that any fast water fly *must* have if it is to gain a lasting popularity. White calf hair wings and tail make the H and L a good one in that respect, particularly when cast from a moving boat. Ask a guide; this fly is often his ace in the hole.

What the H and L imitates and the question why does it seem to work when similar flies like the Royal Wulff fail is an interesting topic of debate among local fishermen. However, for use in small pocket-water streams or during a float trip down the Madison, it always pays to have a few along. We'll let a guide fill you in on why it works, and what it imitates.

As with most hairwings, the H and L is a fairly challenging fly for most tiers. Working with hair causes bulk and proportion problems. Look at the photograph and closely study the proportions, especially the wing position. Since the wing is the first thing tied on, its location affects all other proportions. After the wing the tail is tied on, the butts of which should fit snugly against those of the wing, thus leaving no gaps or bumps where the body will be. The body is tied from a single strand of peacock. Strip a small amount (3/4-1 inch) of the peacock quill free of flues with a thumbnail. Tie in and wind forward; the bare quill should amount to one-half or just a bit more of the total body length, the rest will be unstripped peacock. Hackle in the conventional manner, with two full hackles, and whip finish to form a small head.

H and L Variant

HOOK: Mustad 94840 or equivalent, #10-#18.
THREAD: 6/0 black.
TAIL: White calf body hair.
BODY: Peacock quill, followed by peacock herl.
WING: White calf body hair, upright and divided.
HACKLE: Brown.

Griffith's Gnat

We first read Ernest Schwiebert's *Nymphs* in early 1974—on pages 113 and 114 of our copy a red marking pen highlights the "Griffith's Gnat" story. The pattern named after George Griffith of Michigan, an early pioneer in Trout Unlimited, has become a favorite of ours. There is not a month of the year we do not use the Griffith's Gnat. It works not only during the "smutting rises" so often encountered during Diptera emergences on stillwaters like Hebgen and Quake Lakes, but also imitates the mating clumps of midges encountered on the edges of swift flowing streams like the Madison.

During winter and early spring we are fortunate to be able to fish the Diptera emergences on the Madison. Around 9:00 A.M. these little guys emerge in great numbers. As the numbers of adults build up along the shoreline, the clusters or clumps of mating Diptera become more noticeable. These clumps can be as few as six to eight individuals or as many as a few dozen. We have observed mating clumps as large as a man's fist rolling along the current seams. Fish that attack these clumps slice into them, breaking the large clump up into many smaller clusters. Usually the fish will then drop back and take the smaller clusters which can be imitated very effectively by the Griffith's Gnat in sizes #12 to #14. This hatch can continue as late as 2:00 P.M., even with air temperature as cold as 10 to 15 degrees. The Diptera that leave their two inch micro-habitat of safety at the water's surface will freeze to death. Sometimes the angler who leaves the micro-habitat of his vehicle feels he will freeze to death too.

The original Griffith's Gnat called for a body of peacock with grizzly hackle palmered up the body. While we usually tie our own imitations with this recipe there are times when other combinations are more effective. Try a dark dun hackle and peacock, grizzly hackle and red thread body, brown hackle and olive body, or cream hackle and cream body. For imitating midge clusters imitations in sizes #12 to #18 perform very well.

During the "smutting rise" when fish are taking single emerging Diptera in stillwater situations you will need smaller imitations, sizes #16 to #22.

Tying the Griffith's Gnat is simple. After affixing a hackle to the rear of the hook shank, tie in and wind one or two strands of peacock herl up the hook shank.

Palmer the hackle along the body and tie off at the hook eye. Whip finish and go fishing.

Griffith's Gnat

HOOK: Mustad 94840 or equivalent, #12-#22.
THREAD: 6/0 black.
BODY: Peacock herl.
HACKLE: Grizzly palmered, 4 to 8 turns along the body.

Giant & Summer Crane Fly Larvae

Fly fishermen who enjoy streamside entomology will be most impressed by doing some seining on the Madison River in the Slide Inn to Raynolds Pass area or in any of the side channels from the Slide to Ennis Lake. You will not believe the giant crane fly larvae dredged up in the seine. Dirty olive in color, these babies look like olive link sausages.

The first time we spotted these big uglies was in early winter, 1979. On the way down to fish large stone-fly nymphs at Varney Bridge we decided to seine at Slide Inn to allow more time for the water to warm—it was only 36 degrees. The first dip of the seine revealed 6 to 8 of these giants. Arriving back in West Yellowstone that night we could not wait to find out something of these monsters. Schwiebert's *Nymphs* called them Giant Crane Fly Larva. We tied a few crude imitations on a #2 hook with thirty turns of .025 lead. We really could have used army helmets to protect our heads when casting these bombs to the Madison's browns and rainbows. These large imitations proved very effective, and have since added a lot of weight to our nymph boxes. It seems that the Madison and Henry's Fork rainbows relish these giant *Tipulidae* larvae. For some reason we just do not take that many browns on our imitations unless we drop down to sizes #6-#8. Since rainbows do not seem to mind the smaller sizes and because small imitations are easier to cast and control, our flies are now tied in the #6 to #10 size range.

Another effective crane fly larva pattern for Yellowstone area ponds, sloughs, lakes and streams is the Summer Crane Fly Larva as dubbed by Ernie Schwiebert in *Nymphs.* This gray larva is much smaller than the Giant Crane Fly Larva.

There is a small pond near town that regularly gives up brook trout to 4 pounds on this pattern. We have found this little fly to be very effective in beaver ponds and small lakes simply by casting it out, letting it sink to the bottom, then hand-twist retrieving it back. The fly must be worked *slowly* along the bottom. The fish's take is subtle. It almost always stops the nymph and holds it for just a split second. The set must come quickly on any resistance felt.

Both crane fly patterns are tied the same way. Start by tying in short gills at the hook bend. Attach the gold wire rib, and lay a foundation of lead wire on the shank. Dub a rough body over the lead wire, three-quarters of the hook shank in length. Dub a rough thorax over the remaining hook shank, rib the body with the gold wire, and finish off with a small head.

Giant Crane Fly Larva

HOOK:	Mustad 79580 or equivalent, sizes #6-#10.
THREAD:	6/0 olive.
GILLS:	Dark brown pheasant tail ¼ inch long.
RIB:	Gold wire.
BODY:	Rough dubbed rabbit dyed olive-gold, with the guard hairs in. Dub this over a foundation of .020 lead wire, 25 to 30 turns. We usually put an underbody of olive wool yarn over the lead, this saves much time and effort dubbing larger imitations.

THORAX: Brown Australian opossum or rabbit roughly dubbed and teased out.

Summer Crane Fly Larva

HOOK: Mustad 79580 or equivalent, #10-#14.
THREAD: 6/0 brown.
GILLS: Natural grey-blue pheasant back feather fibers tied on as a short tail.
BODY: Light gray muskrat, with guard hairs.
RIB: Fine gold wire.
THORAX: Medium grey dubbing.

Prince Nymph

Irridescence seems to be the key to nymph patterns using peacock for bodies. One theory goes that peacock gives off light wavelengths that fish can see and man cannot. Whether this is true or not, or even if it is of importance, is unclear. What is clear is that fish love peacock on a fly, and this fly has plenty of it.

We know many guides and fly fishing friends who fish only the Prince Nymph when doing their nymphing. One friend who comes to Yellowstone every August, fishing the last two weeks of the month with #4 to #8 prince nymphs, recently brought one back into the shop—one we had tied for him. He showed us the well-chewed #4 Prince and jokingly complained it had taken "only fourteen fish before all the peacock was torn off it."

Most guides and local fly fishermen floating the Yellowstone, Madison or Bighorn will always be armed with a good selection of Prince Nymphs in sizes #8 to #12. We even know of fly fishermen who use *floating* Prince Nymphs and do well.

This pattern was originally called the Brown Fork Tail and was first tied by Doug Prince in California over forty years ago. It is hard to say how long it has been fished here around Yellowstone but we know shop owners and guides who were recommending and using it before 1970.

We have all known those periods when nothing seems to be happening on the Yellowstone, Madison or Box Canyon of the Henry's Fork: try a #10 or #12 Prince Nymph as the dropper with a #14 Green LaFontaine Caddis Pupa on the point. This combination has worked for us when all else has failed.

To begin tying the Prince nymph attach two tails of brown stripped goose. Weight the hook with wraps of lead wire. Tie in the flat tinsel rib, followed by four or five strands of peacock herl. Wrap the peacock herl forward to the hook eye and tie off. With the tying thread, wrap back to the tail and forward again in a crisscross pattern over the peacock body. This adds durability to the Prince. Wind the tinsel in even spirals up the body and tie off at the eye.

Next tie in the hackle and take one or two wraps. Finally tie in two white horns of stripped goose quill and whip finish.

Prince Nymph

HOOK:	Mustad 9671 or equivalent, #4-#14.
THREAD:	6/0 brown or black.
TAIL:	Stripped brown goose quills.
BODY:	Peacock herl.
RIB:	Fine flat gold or silver tinsel.
HACKLE:	Brown or speckled brown hen hackle.
HORNS:	White stripped goose quills.

Zug Bug

The Zug Bug is another nymph pattern using the irridescence of peacock. Around Yellowstone it is often referred to as the "Old Faithful Nymph" owing to its extreme effectiveness on the Firehole River. What most fishermen do not realize is that it is equally effective on most other rivers, streams, lakes, and ponds.

Never get caught in the trap of thinking that a specific fly works only on a certain river or lake. We know of many instances where a fly created for a specific body of water or hatch situation has worked on almost any other trout water. Cliff Zug had this in mind when he created the Zug Bug so many years ago. He wanted this nymph to have almost universal application.

There have been arguments over the years as to just why trout take the Zug Bug. Perhaps they take it for a damselfly or dragonfly nymph, a Green Drake or a stonefly nymph. Whatever the reason, the trout find the Zug Bug hard to resist.

Our close friend Paul Studebaker swears by the Zug Bug on the Firehole and Madison in Yellowstone Park. Another friend and guide of many years uses it when all else fails on the lower Madison. Some of the older and wiser hands who spend the summers on Hebgen Lake find it very effective in sizes #12 to #14 when used on the cruising rainbows and browns before they turn to dry flies in July and August. Many of these old boys cannot see the small dry flies normally used to match the hatch on Hebgen or Quake Lake so they just keep fishing the Zug Bug with great success.

The Zug Bug is a basic fly to tie; it should pose no problems. One thought in the interest of durability on any peacock bodied fly: wrap the peacock herl around the

the tying thread to form a "rope", then wind this "rope" to make the body. Wrapping the body in this manner increases durability and results in your being able to take twice as many fish before the peacock gives out.

After tying in a tail of peacock sword and a rib of oval silver tinsel, wind a peacock body using the "rope" technique. The body should stop just behind the hook eye. Rib with the tinsel and tie off. Tie in and wrap a soft brown hackle. Next cut a triangular wing case from a mallard duck flank feather. The wingcase is tied on flat over the body at the eye of the hook. Complete the fly with a whip finish.

Zug Bug

HOOK:	Mustad 9671 or equivalent, #8 to #16. Weight if desired.
THREAD:	6/0 black.
TAIL:	Peacock sword fibers.
BODY:	Peacock herl.
RIB:	Oval silver tinsel.
HACKLE:	Brown or speckled brown hen hackle.
WINGCASE:	Trimmed mallard flank feather.

Feather Duster

The Feather Duster is a favorite nymph that was brought to our attention by West Yellowstone resident Wally Eagle. Wally informs us that he first started fishing the Feather Duster on small spring creeks outside Bozeman, Montana, in the early 1970's.

His success prompted him to begin fishing it on the streams around Yellowstone, where it rapidly became a standard pattern. Wally fishes this nymph year-round, and tells us it catches 95% of his nymph-caught trout. It has proven as successful on the Henry's Fork as it has on the Madison and Gallatin Rivers.

The Feather Duster accurately represents many mayfly species, and Wally and his friend Jim Pease frequently fish small Feather Dusters to bank-sipping rainbows on the Railroad Ranch during mayfly hatches. The fly can also suggest damselfly, dragonfly, and little stonefly nymphs.

Every winter we run into Wally fishing the Madison below Quake Lake, and he invariably has a Feather Duster tied to his leader. He invariably has a trout attached to the leader as well. It's always a little peculiar to watch him fishing in the winter, as the rubber dishwashing gloves he wears to keep his hands warm would look more at home in a kitchen sink than on the banks of the Madison.

Wally confessed to us that he has never liked to dub when tying flies, and from that dislike sprung the Feather Duster; it uses ostrich herl instead of dubbing for a body and thorax. The Duster is tied as follows.

After tying on the tail and attaching the wire rib, weight the hook shank with lead wire. Cover the lead wire with wraps of fine wool yarn. This is an important step because the wool yarn acts as a cushion for the delicate ostrich herl, greatly increasing the durability of the fly. Tie in and wind the ostrich herl halfway up the hook shank. Tie it off but do not trim the herl away.

At this point tie in the wingcase material. The length of this material should be equal to the wingcase length plus the leg length. This is critical, because the legs will be formed from the tied down ends of the wingcase. Wind the ostrich herl forward to form a thorax, and tie off behind the hook eye. Trim the butts. Wind the wire rib along the entire body and tie off at the hook eye. Pull the wingcase down over the thorax and tie down tightly. Take the remaining ends of the wingcase, divide them equally, pull them back alongside the thorax on either side and tie down, forming the legs. Complete the fly with a whip finish.

Feather Duster

HOOK:	Mustad 9672 or equivalent, sizes #10-#16.
THREAD:	6/0 brown or olive.
TAIL:	For size #12 and larger, pheasant tail fibers.
	For size #14 and smaller, partridge fibers.
BODY:	Natural ostrich herl.
RIB:	Fine copper wire.
WINGCASE:	For size #12 and larger, pheasant tail fibers.
	For size #14 and smaller, partridge fibers.
LEGS:	Formed from the wingcase fibers.

Hare's Ear

The Hare's Ear is to nymph fishermen what the Adams is to dry fly fishermen: the preeminent fly, the virtuoso performer. The Hare's Ear needs no justification or long elaboration of its qualities, and we don't pretend to have much new to say about it. It is simply one of the quintessential Yellowstone nymphs. It is fished everywhere and catches fish everywhere.

Just what does the Hare's Ear represent? Nothing in particular, but everything in general. In fact, F.M. Halford, the strict imitationist of nineteenth century dry fly men, totally gave up the use of the dry Hare's Ear despite his once great advocacy of it, presumably because he could not explain his success with it. It worked at times when it should have been a dismal failure. Though Halford was referring to the dry Hare's Ear, his point is well taken and equally applicable to the nymph. We don't, however, recommend giving up the use of the fly simply because of the lack of a "theory of imitation"!

There is nothing complicated about tying the Hare's Ear, though for some reason it is a hard pattern for many tiers to proportion properly. After tying in a short tail, one third the length of the shank, attach the gold tinsel and then thinly dub the body. Many tiers get in trouble here by extending the body too far forward and ending up with an anemic thorax. The body should stop in the middle of the hook—no farther. Wind the gold rib. Tie in the wingcase, dub the thorax, then pull over and tie off the wingcase at the eye. The thorax should be just about half the length of the fly, minus the tail. This closely approximates the proportions of most natural nymphs.

Hare's Ear

HOOK: Mustad 3906 or equivalent, #8-#18, weighted.
THREAD: 6/0 brown.
BODY: Hare's ear dubbing.
TAIL: Hare's ear fur, just a pinch.
RIB: Fine flat gold tinsel.
THORAX: Hare's ear dubbing, roughly dubbed.
WINGCASE: Mottled turkey, optional.

Soft Hackles

The soft hackle is not a fly pattern *per se,* but rather a class of patterns all based on similar tying principles. They are simple flies, typically nothing more than a thread body occasionally dubbed with fur, and a wrap or two of "soft" hackle at the head. Soft hackles can be tied to imitate specific insects or to suggest a genre of insects, such as caddis pupa or mayfly emergers.

It is surprising to us that soft hackles have not had more of an impact in the Yellowstone area, but it is also understandable, considering several stereotypes unnecessarily draped upon them. First is the misconception that because of their ancient Scottish ancestry they are simply outdated or that they aren't applicable to American waters. While it's true that many existing patterns aren't reasonable imitations of our trout stream insects, this is no reason for the progressive fisherman to forsake their use. In fact, this is probably the crux of the issue: there has been almost no effort to correlate American hatches with appropriate soft hackle patterns. As for being outdated, one need only fish these simple patterns to find out how inaccurate that criticism is.

Second, it is commonly thought that soft hackles must be fished down and across stream on a taut line. It is unfortunate that so many fishermen are under this impression, because down and across is just one option. The soft hackle is often deadliest when fished upstream, drag-free, to individual feeding fish. It is a more difficult technique because of the problems of avoiding drag and sensing the take (there is rarely the solid pull of the kind the down and across cast yields), but fishing them this way opens up many more possibilities for the use of these flies. Flies unable to swim or swim well (many mayfly nymphs and emergers for instance) can be imitated and fished, as well as more active flies like caddis pupae.

Soft hackles are uncomplicated flies, but properly tying these simple, sparse patterns requires some thought. Attach the Pearsall's tying thread directly behind the eye of the hook, and tie on the hackle first, facing out over the hook eye. Smoothly wrap the thread halfway to two-thirds down the hook shank and back up to just behind the hackle. Leave no gaps and create no lumps in the body. Now, very sparsely dub the tying thread—just enough for a wrap or two. Note the photograph. Wind the dubbing on and advance thread in front of the hackle. Take one, or at the very most two, wraps of hackle and tie off. Tying on the hackle first and winding it last contributes greatly to maintaining a slim, spartan fly. Cement the head; Pearsall's silk is unwaxed so the head should be sealed.

Soft Hackles

Three Yellowstone favorites:

Ephemerella Nymph

HOOK: Mustad 3906 or 94840 (for dry or semi-dry version) or equivalents, #14-#20.
THREAD: Pearsall's brown silk.
BODY: Pearsall's brown silk.
THORAX: Brown hare's ear dubbing.
HACKLE: Brown partridge, one turn.

Caddis emerger (Brachycentrus sp.)

HOOK: Mustad 3906 or 94840 or equivalents, #14-#16.
THREAD: Green Pearsall's silk.
BODY: Green Pearsall's silk, very lightly dubbed with gray antron, allowing the silk color to show through.
THORAX: Same as body.
HACKLE: Moorhen or Snipe, one turn.

Pale Morning Dun emerger

HOOK: Mustad 94840 or equivalent, #16-#18.
THREAD: Yellow Pearsall's silk.
BODY: Yellow Pearsall's silk, lightly dubbed with chocolate fur, allowing silk color to show through.
THORAX: Chocolate dubbing.
HACKLE: Golden plover, one turn.

Midge Pupa

The spring creeks of Paradise Valley are uncluttered places during the months of March and April. The creek bottoms have a gaunt look, much as the deer that inhabit them do, if the winter was particularly severe.

The trees are barren of leaves and the grasses that will somehow flourish in two months are dead and decaying. The creeks themselves are skeletons; gone with winter are the lush weed beds that once sheltered both fish and fly. Vegetation seems to hold a spring creek together, and without it there is a funny sense of emptiness, particularly on a creek you have seen in full bloom. There are also few fishermen to contend with.

The fish are still there, both the browns and rainbows, and they are actively feeding too. They seem more obvious now, perhaps because of the lack of vegetation. Their rises are mostly to midge pupae, and they will feed all day as the flies straggle off. The *Baetis* mayflies have begun hatching also, but are only present for a few hours each day. The midges are the main fare, and will continue to be for many weeks.

To really be successful in this situation and others like it in Yellowstone, fishing the pupal stage of the midge is the best plan. The dry adult will always have its place in the sun, especially if the midges are clumping up and drifting during mating, but during an actual emergence (whether it be on a spring creek, Hebgen Lake, or the Henry's Fork river), trout will generally concentrate on emerging pupae. The drifting pupae area easy pickings for a trout because there is no real chance of their escape. A fully emerged adult can take to the air anytime, and in the delicate balance of energy expended for energy gained, a trout can't afford to miss too many of these little flies before the scale tips the wrong way.

Fishing midge pupae in rivers usually calls for dead drift tactics, but on the lakes around here an active presentation often works best. On Hebgen and Quake Lakes, casting in front of a cruising trout and drawing the pupa slowly and steadily across his path is a deadly technique. So, too, is the tactic of hitting them right on the head with the fly; we use this occasionally when it seems the fish are actually ignoring our patterns. The unfortunate consequence of this tactic is that a bad cast usually means a spooked trout!

The midge pupa we favor in an uncomplicated pattern. A spartan body of thinly dubbed antron, followed by a turn of starling hackle and a final turn or two of darker dubbing is all there is to it. Besides mimicking the sparseness of natural pupae, there is a latent reason for the simple dressing. That is to avoid use of excess materials that might cause the fly to float. We like the pupa to hit the water and immediately enter the surface film, exactly where the fish expect to find the naturals.

Midge Pupa

HOOK:	Mustad 94840 or equivalent, #14-#22.
THREAD:	6/0 black.
BODY:	Antron dubbing, extending down on to hook bend, in olive, black, green, or red.
HACKLE:	One turn of starling.
HEAD:	One or two turns of dark dubbing.

Yellowstone Scud

An often overlooked pattern, this one produces very fine results. The scud is a pattern which comes in all flavors and, as with most patterns, the simpler the tie the more effective the fly. We prefer orangish pink, olive, and gray colors for our imitations. We also like to use antron dubbings or natural seal in tying the scud, as both materials are highly translucent.

For several years, we had just about forgotten about scuds even though we had always had tremendous success with them. Then one day while fishing a local slough that Nick Lyons named "Tortuga Bay" we found an orangish pink scud hanging in a nearby bush. The original owner had apparently lost his fly on a backcast and since we had been skunked, we looked upon this fly as a positive omen.

A pair of osprey watched from their perch over the Bay as we knotted the fly to the tippet. Since no tortugas could be seen cruising we sat on the bank, had lunch and waited. Soon a cruiser swam within six feet of us, rooting and tailing in the mud after nymphs and scuds as it worked its way up the shoreline. The fish's tail looked wider than a canoe paddle. After casting the scud upstream of the fish we allowed it to sink to the bottom. As he approached within a foot of our fly we slowly lifted it. The fish's mouth opened and closed in a wink of white. You would have thought we were fishing tarpon with fifty pound tippet the way we struck with our 5x. Our new found scud, hooked tortuga, and two feet of tippet swam out of sight.

Returning to our vises later that day we tied several scud imitations, vowing never to be without this pattern again.

Fly fishermen planning to fish lakes, ponds, spring creeks or tail waters should have several of these flies in their arsenal. Last April on the Bighorn we fished scuds exclusively as we were too early for good *Baetis* hatches. Three of us had great fishing for browns in the 14 to 22 inch class on this scud imitation.

We have tried tying and fishing this pattern with and without a shell back strip cut from a poly bag. For some reason it seems that the scud tied with the shellback takes more fish—maybe we fish them harder or with more faith but it is true that we do better with those flies tied with a shellback.

First cut a narrow strip of poly bag material and tie it in at the rear of the hook, along with fine gold wire. Weight the hook shank with lead wire. Roughly dub a body of seal or antron dubbing to behind the hook eye. Pull the poly strip over the top of the body and tie off at the eye. Wind the gold wire rib forward in even turns and fasten securely. Finally, pick out the dubbing on the sides and bottom of the fly with a bodkin.

Yellowstone Scud

HOOK: Mustad 3906 or equivalent, #8-#16.
THREAD: 6/0 orange or olive.
SHELLBACK: Poly bag strip.
RIB: Fine gold wire.
BODY: Orangish pink or olive antron or seal dubbing, picked out on sides and bottom.

Woolhead Sculpin

Because sculpins are the most common baitfish in the rivers of Yellowstone, an appropriate imitation is a must for your streamer box. There are dozens of different styles to choose from, all of which will catch fish, but we prefer the woolhead variety for several reasons.

Many of the sculpin patterns currently popular are tied with deer hair heads, spun and then trimmed to resemble the broad, flat head that the naturals sport. Though deer makes a beautiful head, it also floats very well and sculpins are usually more effective on the bottom. This can be offset by heavily weighting the fly, but it then becomes a rather hazardous thing to cast.

Wool sinks well, is simpler to use, and is very suggestive, which is why we use it in place of deer for sculpin heads. For sculpins designed to be fished on the bottom woolhead flies require less weighting and are consequently easier to cast and fish. Wool is also very translucent and looks more "alive" than deer hair. For fly tiers wool is a far easier material to work with than deer, because it doesn't need to be "spun" to create a head.

On certain occasions we want our sculpin imitations to ride much higher in the water, for instance, when fishing shallow water or for periods just before dark, when a dead drifted sculpin right under the surface is kill-ing. In these situations, a woolhead imitation tied with no weight at all is perfect. They sink just the right amount.

No one knows who first used wool as a substitute for deer. The patterns have been around for many years, but only in the last three or four have they started to catch on with fishermen. Besides the natural olive sculpin color, they are deadly attractors when dressed in solid black and pure white.

To tie the woolhead sculpin proceed as follows. Tie in a length of wool yarn for the body along with a section of gold wire that will be used as a rib. Weight the hook, if desired, with lead wire wound over the tied down yarn butts. Wind the wool yarn to form the body, leaving the front quarter of the shank exposed. Tie in a strip of rabbit fur long enough to reach past the bend of the hook, where the body ends. Bind the fur strip down matuka style with the gold rib. Attach two sage grouse feathers, one on each side, to simulate pectoral fins.

Forming the wool head to finish the fly is quite simple. First lay a Monocord base on the exposed hook shank. Wool is slippery, and since it won't be spun ala deer hair it needs something to bite into and anchor on. Cut a clump of wool about the diameter of a pencil from the hide. With the clump facing either way, slide it directly over the hook eye to the point where the head will start. The wool should completely encircle the hook. Bind down the middle of the clump at the point where the head starts with five tight wraps of Monocord. Pull the front half of the clump back and take several tight wraps in front of it. This firmly anchors it to the hook. Pull the front ends back again and secure additional clumps of wool to finish the head. Depending on their thickness, it should take two or three more clumps. Whip finish and trim the head with sharp scissors to a sculpin-like resemblance. Leave some wool trailing to form a collar.

Woolhead Scuplin

HOOK: Mustad 9672, 79580 or equivalent, #2-#8.
THREAD: 3/0 Monocord, brown.

BODY:	Olive wool yarn.
RIB:	Gold wire.
WING:	Strip of rabbit fur, light olive.
FINS:	Sage grouse feathers dyed olive.
COLLAR AND HEAD:	Clumps of wool, bound to the hook shank and trimmed. We like to mottle the head using different colors of wool, e.g. olive, brown, and gray.

Soft Hackle Streamer

How about a fly that costs around a nickel in materials, takes less than five minutes to tie, sinks well with no additional weight, is extremely durable and catches fish like there's no tomorrow? Such a fly is the Soft Hackle Streamer, introduced to us by our friend Jack Gartside. Jack has always liked flies that are "pretty to look at and fun to tie" in addition to being very effective.

During the past two years this fly has been a top producer for us at ice-out in May on Quake and Hebgen Lakes as well as in the fall while spawner fishing on the Madison, Gallatin and Yellowstone. Paul Studebaker took a brown of twenty-seven inches and Jim Yerrick a rainbow "over" twenty-six inches on Soft Hackle Streamers this past fall, both in the Madison above Hebgen Lake. Fishing an olive and black Soft Hackle Streamer we caught and released over 25 browns and rainbows in one afternoon across from the boat launch on Quake Lake late last May. We arrived at 3:00 P.M. and fished the 40 to 50 feet of water between shore and the remaining ice pack. Our most effective casts were those that fell on the ice; we would then pull the fly off the ice flow and allow it to sink a few feet before stripping the fly back in short rapid strips. The takes were vicious that afternoon and without shock gum in the leader we would have lost many more flies and fish than we did. Our best fish was a nineteen inch brown—no monster, but a wonderful fish to start out our lake fishing season.

We use different colored Soft Hackle Streamers for different fishing circumstances. Fall brown trout in their spawning mode seem to prefer the yellow, black, or olive colors. Rainbows tagging along with these fall spawning browns prefer white or olive/black.

Use blood marabou or marabou shorts in tying this pattern. Begin the tying by attaching two pieces of flashabou midway up the hook shank. Next tie in a marabou plume by the butt in front of the flashabou. Wrap two or three turns of the marabou forward just as one would a hackle. Tie the plume off and, if tying a two-color pattern, attach and wrap the other marabou plume. The next step is to tie in and wind one turn of a mallard flank feather. One side of this feather should be stripped of its fibers before tying in and winding. If this is not done the fibers have a tendency to splay wildly instead of lying closely along the marabou wing.

No additional weight is required for this pattern. Due to the nature of materials used, once the marabou and mallard become wet it sinks well. As a matter of fact we fish the Soft Hackle Streamer on a floating line, letting it sink from 6 to 24 inches before starting a rapid erratic retrieve. Part of the enjoyment in fishing this fly is to watch a big brown or rainbow come off the bottom like a rocket to intercept the fly just as you start your retrieve. We will bet you pull the fly right away from the fish the first two or three times this happens.

Soft Hackle Streamer

HOOK: Mustad 3906, #4-#6.
THREAD: 3/0 red, white, yellow, black. Use a thread color to contrast with the marabou wing, not complement it.

TAIL: Two silver strands of Flashabou or pearl Crystal Hair.

BODY: None.

WING: Blood marabou wound as a hackle. Most popular colors are: black, olive, yellow, white, and black/olive. The wing is followed by a turn of mallard flank feather dyed to match the marabou.

Wooly Bugger

Originally an eastern fly that was transplanted to the west, the Wooly Bugger is probably the most popular streamer used in Yellowstone country. The marabou and palmered hackle give the fly an excellent action, one that a competent fisherman can enhance even further with a good retrieve.

The Wooly Bugger is a fly for all angling seasons; spring, summer, fall, and even winter. Starting early it is an excellent choice for fishing the lakes just after ice-out. Cast from shore and stripped back rapidly it has accounted for many hungry browns and rainbows. In the summer it can stir things up on an otherwise slow day, fished dead drift or actively retrieved down a riffle. On overcast days it is a favorite choice of the guides during a float trip. A summer evening on a small creek or pond is a great time to fish a Wooly Bugger.

Fall is perhaps the best season for applying the Bugger though. The browns and rainbows start to feel the spawning urge and become aggressive and territorial. A rapid retrieve through their holding water will evoke a hectic chase and, more often than not, a vicious strike. Aside from the standard black and olive, bright yellow is a hard color to beat for these spawners. In fact, our favorite time to fish the Wooly Bugger is late fall on the upper Madison, casting the bright yellow flies across and downstream and stripping them back just under the surface. In the smooth stretches of the upper river it is easy to see the fish giving chase, and the faster the retrieve the faster they come, until finally we stop the retrieve dead in its track, forcing the fish to make a play. Nine times out of ten it manifests itself as a slashing strike.

The most important material for tying the Wooly Bugger is good, fluffy marabou. Most tiers prefer the soft, short "blood" feathers that can be used whole. The actual tying is not difficult at all. Begin by tying on the marabou tail. Then tie in a length of chenille and a saddle hackle (this should be tied in by the tip), both at the rear of the body. Wind the chenille forward, tie it off, and then palmer the hackle in nice, even turns to the head. Tie it off, form a nice head and whip finish.

Wooly Bugger

HOOK: Mustad 9672, 79580 or equivalent, #2-#12.
THREAD: 3/0 Monocord, color to match body.
TAIL: Marabou.
BODY: Chenille.
HACKLE: Saddle hackle, palmered along body. Our favorite colors are solid black, bright yellow, and black and olive (black hackle and marabou, olive body).

Leech

Fly fishermen planning to fish lakes or ponds in Yellowstone country should not be without a few leeches. Simple patterns such as a marabou tail and body, marabou tail with leech yarn body or, even simpler yet, a leech yarn body frizzed out all produce well.

We have found size and, at times, color to be very important. Olive, bright green, brown, black or combinations of these colors seem to produce best from ice-out to July. From August to November purple, crimson, gold and grey give best results. If you are tying your own make sure you have at the very least one dark pattern such as black and one lighter such as gold or light purple. Also have leeches in several sizes from #2 to #14. While we do not suggest you have leeches in each size slot we would recommend at least a few #2, #6, #10, and #14's for instance. It seems there are times when fish can get as selective on leeches as they do on mayflies.

On lakes such as Henry's, Cliff, or Wade, fish will take larger leech imitations during the first month or so of open season. As the summer wears on the angler must go to smaller imitations. By the end of season we are fishing #12 and #14 imitations.

Most tiers tend to overdress leech imitations. We cannot stress enough that the sparser the leech tie, the more effective your pattern will be.

The largest brown and cutthroat trout we have taken were on leech imitations. A twenty-eight inch brown fell to a #8 brown marabou leech and a twenty-six inch cutthroat took a purple leech. Both were taken in small, leech infested sloughs.

It usually requires some time and effort to get the hang of fishing leech imitations. Judging the proper depth, speed, and style of retrieve to use only comes from experimentation. Different days on the same waters can require completely different tactics, and it's not until you are out fishing that the choice for the day becomes clear.

Fly tiers should always keep their leeches simple. Three effective patterns are: 1. A tail of marabou and a body formed by wrapping the butt end of the plume used for the tail up to the eye. Whip finish and you are ready to fish. 2. A tail of marabou and a body of leech yarn wrapped to the hook eye and tied off. 3. Wrap leech yarn on the hook shank, then tease out with a dubbing teaser; that's it!